CANDLE*79 COOKBOOK

CANDLE*79
COOKBOOK

Modern Vegan Classics
from New York's Premier
Sustainable Restaurant

Joy Pierson, Angel Ramos, and Jorge Pineda

FOREWORD BY RORY FREEDMAN

Photography by Rita Maas

TEN SPEED PRESS
Berkeley

In celebration of Jesus Ramos,
Petrona Pineda, Anne Pierson,
Jane Erdman, Minerva Felenstein,
and Ann Marie Chiappetta,
who taught us that food is love.

CONTENTS

xi   Foreword

1   Introduction

Amuse-Bouches and Appetizers   5

6   Heirloom Tomato–Avocado Tartare

9   Roasted Artichokes with Spring Vegetables and
     Crispy Onion Rings

11   Avocado Salsa

12   Zucchini Blossom Tempura

15   Arancini with Roasted Plum
     Tomato Sauce

17   Smoked Paprika Hummus

18   Cashew Cheese–Stuffed Yuca Cakes

19   Spinach-Mushroom Pâté

20   Seitan Cakes

23   Ginger-Seitan Dumplings

Soups   25

26   Live Avocado-Cucumber Soup

29   Farmers' Market Gazpacho

30   Tortilla Soup

33   Jerusalem Artichoke Soup with Crispy Sage Leaves

34   Herbed Potato-Leek Soup

35   Black Bean and Roasted Poblano Soup

36   Butternut Squash–Chestnut Soup
     with Caramelized Pears

Salads   39

40   Heirloom Tomato Salad with Macadamia Cheese
     and Crispy Capers

42   Butterhead Lettuce, Cauliflower, and
     Red Bell Pepper Salad

43   Watercress, Jicama, and Corn Salad
with Jalapeño Dressing

45   Wild Mushroom and Cipollini Salad
with Fresh Horseradish Dressing

46   Kale, Vegetable, and Spelt Berry Salad
with Chive Vinaigrette

48   Stuffed Avocado with Quinoa Pilaf and
Chipotle-Avocado Dressing

49   Seaweed Salad with Ginger-Sesame Dressing

50   Beet, Fennel, and Fig Salad
with Cranberry-Sage Dressing

52   Blood Orange–Fennel Salad

53   Mediterranean Salad with Kalamata
Olive Vinaigrette

Entrées   55

58   Stuffed Poblano Peppers

61   Spring Vegetable Risotto

63   Wild Mushroom and Spring Vegetable Fricassee

64   Herb-Marinated Grilled Vegetables

66   Moroccan-Spiced Chickpea Cakes

69   Saffron Ravioli with Wild Mushrooms
and Cashew Cheese

71   Manicotti Rustica

73   Potato Gnocchi

75   Pan-Seared Pine Nut Pesto Tofu

76   Chile-Grilled Tofu with Avocado-Tomatillo Sauce

78   Live Lasagna

80   Tempeh Cakes

83   Tempeh with Mole Sauce

84   Nori- and Sesame-Crusted Seitan

86   Panko-Crusted Seitan Milanese

87   Sofrito-Seared Seitan

89   Seitan Piccata

90   Tamarind-Barbecued Seitan

91   Paella

94   Spaghetti and Seitan Wheatballs with Roasted Plum
Tomato Sauce

95   Black Bean–Chipotle Burgers

Sides, Sauces, and Secrets 99

100 Barbecued Black-Eyed Peas

101 Granny Smith Coleslaw

101 Sweet Potato Mash

102 Roasted Fingerling Potatoes

103 Potato Cakes

104 Polenta Fries

105 Soba Noodles

106 Jasmine Rice

107 Quinoa-Vegetable Pilaf

108 Marinated Tempeh

109 Seitan Cutlets

110 Sautéed Royal Trumpet Mushrooms

111 Braised Green Beans

112 Gingered Sugar Snap Peas

113 Sautéed Swiss Chard

114 Creamed Spinach

115 Ginger-Soy Dipping Sauce

116 Roasted Plum Tomato Sauce

117 Red Bell Pepper–Curry Sauce

119 Roasted Red Bell Pepper and Tomato Sauce

120 Mint-Cilantro Chimichurri Sauce

121 Pesto

122 Zucchini Blossom Sauce

124 Edamame-Mint Sauce

125 Apricot Chutney

125 Cashew Crème Fraîche

126 Sage or Tarragon Aioli

Brunch 129

130 Chickpea Crepes

131 Wild Mushroom, Asparagus, and Spring Vegetable Crepes

133 Butternut Squash, Mushroom, and Sage Crepes

134 Home-Style Pancakes with Blueberry Butter

136 Sourdough French Toast

137 Tofu and Seitan Sausage Scramble

138 Mixed-Grain Waffles with Raspberry Butter

Desserts 141

142   Summer Berry Crumble
144   Vanilla Bean Ice Cream
145   Chocolate Ice Cream
146   Sorbets
148   Mexican Chocolate Cake
149   Apple-Apricot Strudel
151   Peach Parfait
152   Doughnuts
154   Chocolate Mousse Tower

Drinks 157

158   Apricot Spritzer
159   Elderberry Elixir
160   Ginger Ale
163   Coconut-Mint Frappé
165   Summer Sangria
166   Winter Spiced Sangria
167   Cherry Pie
168   Pomegranate Cosmo
169   Mango Margarita
170   French 79
172   The Grapevine
173   Ginger Rush
174   Sake Mojito Classico
174   Mixed Berry Sake Mojito
176   Cucumber-Basil Martini

179   Glossary
182   Resources
185   Acknowledgments
187   About the Authors
188   Index
193   Measurement Conversion Charts

FOREWORD

When I first went vegetarian, then vegan, I did so begrudgingly. Eating is my favorite thing to do above all else; I did not want to forgo any earthly pleasures. But when I made the connection—*animal products equal cruelty*—I vowed never to contribute to the suffering of animals again. And at first, kicking my meat, cheese, and egg addictions was a challenge. And at times, it felt like a sacrifice.

I had been vegetarian for ten years, and was newly vegan, when I first set foot inside the sanctum of Candle 79. It was literally like nothing I had ever experienced. There were no sacrifices here! This was upscale fare, as indulgent as anything I'd eaten as a meathead. Chimichurris, seitan piccata, risotto, ravioli—to this day, every time I go to the restaurant, I lose my mind. I'm a foodie. I want every meal I eat to be orgasmic. Candle 79 has never disappointed.

Chefs Angel and Jorge are geniuses who somehow achieve the impossible—everything is really hearty, hale, and decadent, but also really light and fresh. I know part of that has to do with the seasonal, local, organic produce they use. Another element is magic. Sheer magic. The final component is pretty simple: They all care. Owners Joy and Bart want to feed us the best meals possible, made from the best stuff possible, while being as conscientious and eco-minded as possible.

Their love is evident everywhere in the restaurant. There's no pretension or stuffiness despite the opulent decor, perfect presentation, and impeccable service. Joy and Bart did more than create a haven for foodies—they created a community. Their staff is their family. And their clientele is comprised of everyone—power brokers, punk rockers, doctors, lawyers, yogis, celebrities, everyone in between, and even restaurateurs and top chefs. Not only do we want their food, we also want what they have. We want that spark, spirit, and love.

This book is so clearly a labor of love. Every single recipe is mouth-watering. And they all reflect what Bart and Joy set out to do with their restaurants: They show us that we can eat amazing food, take excellent care of our bodies, and respect Mother Earth and all her inhabitants. And that none of that ever means having to sacrifice anything. This cookbook is a celebration. A celebration of what vegan cuisine can and should be.

When Joy and Bart decided to share their passion for vegan food with the world, they won $53,000 in the New York Lottery, which helped them get started. One of their favorite mottos (paraphrased from Goethe) sums it up perfectly: "When you commit, providence will provide." So whether you want to spare animals, save the planet, better your health, or just enjoy great food, somehow your path led you here, to this book.

For me, veganism is the perfect expression of all those things. It's the doorway to better everything: Health, energy, longevity, compassion, consciousness, and connectedness. Mind, body, spirit, and the best food on the planet. Veganism really is a noble pursuit. (Except for the part where you're constantly mowing down food in a breathless state of gluttony. That's not noble, it's just a bonus.) Being vegan is what I'm most proud of. And to contribute to this book is such an honor.

About two years after Candle 79 opened, I moved to the West Coast, three thousand miles away from the beloved mecca. So this cookbook makes my soul sing. It's a cornucopia of epic proportions and excitement. And it's an extension of the generosity that abounds at the restaurant—the notion that good, healthy food should be lavished on everyone, and that every bite should taste absolutely divine. Joy, Angel, and Jorge have poured their beautiful, kind, committed hearts into this book. They leave nothing to be desired. It's all here.

I'm committed to feasting on every single recipe in this book. And providence has provided me with friends who are as enthusiastic about food as I am. I foresee many Candle 79 potlucks in my immediate future. And I'm struck by how the spirit and abundance of Candle 79 continues to grow.

Rory Freedman, coauthor of *Skinny Bitch* and *Skinny Bitch in the Kitch*

Mushrooms (top left clockwise to center): Cauliflower, Oyster, Chanterelle, Hen of the Woods (or Maitake), Matsutake, Lobster, Bluefoot, Chicken of the Woods, Shiitake, Morel

INTRODUCTION

Since its inception in 2003, Candle 79 has become a New York institution, a destination for vegan, vegetarian, and omnivore diners alike. Because our food tastes so delicious and is so healthy, our customers are constantly asking for recipes from the restaurant to cook at home for their loved ones and to celebrate every occasion.

The food at Candle 79 expands the horizons of vegan cuisine, proving that the healthiest food can also be the most flavorful and satisfying. Seeing the power and effect that our food has on those who dine with us compelled us to take it a step further. Our mission was to create the best possible cuisine for our friends, our customers, and the growing audience of people from all over the world who are committed to eating and living well but can't dine with us in person. The recipes in the *Candle 79 Cookbook* are from the kitchen's repertoire and have been tested and tailored for the home cook. We hope they will bring the magic of dining at Candle 79 into your home for making everyday meals as well as dishes for special celebrations.

Our History

In the 1980s, the restaurant's founder, Bart Potenza, bought and operated a landmark juice bar and vitamin shop named Sunny's on the Upper East Side of Manhattan. He renamed it Healthy Candle after the previous owners' charming ritual of lighting candles all over the store to bless their establishment. Little did he know at the time that he was creating an enterprise that would feed and nurture thousands of people for the next twenty-six years (and counting). He met Joy Pierson, a nutritionist, in 1987, and they soon became business and life partners. Over the years, they became a powerful team in the vegetarian and holistic movement and sought to expand their restaurant business. As luck would have it, in August, 1993, they won

$53,000 in the New York Lottery on a single ticket that was purchased on Friday the thirteenth. That win provided the seed money to open Candle Cafe. The restaurant became a hit, serving organic vegan food from the freshest local ingredients available. The growth of this mission-driven business led to the creation of a booming catering enterprise, a wholesale line of foods, the *Candle Cafe Cookbook*, and the birth of Candle 79.

Candle 79

In 2003, demand for growth called again, and Candle 79 was born five blocks away from the cafe. This time, the Candle's famed organic vegan cuisine was presented in a different setting, a two-story fine dining oasis with an elegant bar that serves organic wine, beer, sake, and spirits for the conscientious yet sophisticated eater. The acclaimed chefs who created the cuisine at Candle Cafe—Angel Ramos and Jorge Pineda—joined forces with Bart and Joy to launch the restaurant, and their inventive dishes continue to grace its tables. Candle 79 rapidly became a destination restaurant with a stellar reputation. It was selected as Zagat's top-rated vegetarian restaurant in 2007 and 2008 and was the first vegetarian restaurant to be reviewed by Frank Bruni of the *New York Times*. It is the regular restaurant of choice for local families and tourists, as well as celebrities, politicians, and CEOs. All are warmly welcomed as good friends at Candle 79.

Combining creative, elegantly presented, healthy, and delicious cuisine with knowledgeable service, Candle 79 is at the forefront of a movement to bring sophistication to vegetarian cuisine, and to bring the concepts of local, seasonal, sustainable, and vegan into the culinary mainstream.

The Candle commitment extends far beyond the dining room and into the community. The restaurants and their staff have always been focused on putting their passions into action toward building a more unified and sustainable planet. Candle has formed many long-standing partnerships with like-minded organizations and charities to further the reach of their shared missions. Throughout their history, the Candles have been privileged to work with such incredible groups as New York Coalition for Healthy School Food (NYCHSF), People for the Ethical Treatment of Animals (PETA), the Humane Society of the United States (HSUS), Green America, Physicians Committee for Responsible Medicine (PCRM), the Northeast Organic Farming Association (NOFA), and numerous animal shelters and farm sanctuaries, including Farm Sanctuary and Woodstock Farm Sanctuary.

Our Philosophy, Our Book

At Candle 79 we are dedicated to promoting healthy eating through our commitment to plant-based cuisine. Our restaurant's creations are comprised of a seasonal array of organic foods that are grown without the use of pesticides and other chemicals. By supporting organic farming and avoiding the use of animal products, we acknowledge the interconnectedness of physical, spiritual, and environmental well-being. Candle 79 incorporates this spirit by serving great food that comes fresh from farm to table in a serene and seductive atmosphere. We love and support the farmers who have delivered their produce to our restaurant's kitchen year after year, making it possible for us to offer the freshest and most nutrient-dense food available.

We believe that everyone has an inner chef, and the purpose of this book is to awaken that chef and introduce you to the techniques, nuances, and infinite possibilities of plant-based cuisine. Join us in the exploration of the plant kingdom. We want to inspire you to take the plunge into changing the way you think about buying, preparing, and eating food. We have compiled simple-to-follow, delicious, and inspiring recipes for you to create and enjoy in your own kitchen. In addition, there is a glossary to help you understand terms and ingredients used throughout the book, and a resource guide with excellent information on where to find special products that may not be available in mainstream markets.

Plant-based food, enhanced by organic ingredients, has become a necessity for the planet and the health and well-being of the people who occupy it. The cuisine we share with you has the power to reduce your carbon footprint for the benefit of present and future generations. Truly green cuisine is everyone's birthright. Now, with the help and guidance of the *Candle 79 Cookbook*, many more people will have access to our recipes, sources, and restaurant secrets enabling them to create and enjoy delicious dishes in their own homes for themselves and their families and friends. We invite you on this journey to a healthier planet and a healthier you!

So, read on, learn more about cooking the magnificent and delicious array of plant-based foods, and embrace this exciting cuisine.

In Food We Trust,
Joy, Angel, and Jorge

Amuse-Bouches and Appetizers

At Candle 79, we have developed an array of amuse-bouches and appetizers to amuse the palate and tantalize the taste buds. You can create these dishes at home and serve them as a first course or as small bites from a buffet or passed-around trays. Whether made for a family meal, a special-occasion dinner, or a cocktail party, they are always welcome treats and pair beautifully with wine and drinks. From savory, nutty-flavored roasted artichokes and crunchy, bite-sized arancini to simple avocado salsa and homemade hummus, these healthy, tasty bites are great fun to make and share with loved ones, friends, and family.

Heirloom Tomato–Avocado Tartare

This vibrant tartare, made with a raw mushroom ceviche, avocados, and ripe, juicy heirloom tomatoes, pops with all the tastes of summer. It is wonderful as an appetizer served with tortilla chips or crackers (our favorite is raw flaxseed crackers) or as a side dish for a summer barbecue. It's very popular with raw food enthusiasts and carnivores alike.

¼ pound oyster mushrooms, diced
1 shallot, thinly sliced
3 scallions, white and green parts,
　　thinly sliced
3 tablespoons extra-virgin olive oil
Juice of 2 lemons
Sea salt and freshly ground pepper
1 pound heirloom tomatoes, seeded
　　and diced
2 ripe avocados
2 cucumbers, peeled, halved,
　　seeded, and cut into ¼-inch dice
Tortilla strips, for garnish
　　(see page 30)
Sprouts or microgreens, for garnish

Serves 4 to 6

In a small bowl, combine the mushrooms, shallot, scallions, olive oil, 2 tablespoons of the lemon juice, and salt and pepper to taste.

Put the tomatoes in a large bowl. Halve the avocados. Carefully press the blade of a sharp knife into the pit, twist, and pull gently to remove. Cut ¼-inch slices horizontally and vertically into the flesh of the avocados to make medium-sized squares. Scoop out the flesh with a large spoon and add it to the tomatoes, along with the diced cucumbers.

Add the mushroom mixture and the remaining lemon juice to the tomato mixture. Gently mix with a large spoon, making sure not to mash the avocado. Taste and adjust the seasonings if necessary. Cover and chill in the refrigerator for 30 minutes to 1 hour.

To serve, present the tartare in a bowl. You can also offer individual servings: pack the tartare into a 2-inch ring mold to shape it, then remove the mold. Garnish with the tortilla strips and sprouts and serve at once.

Roasted Artichokes with Spring Vegetables and Crispy Onion Rings

This recipe celebrates spring and all it has to offer—warm breezes, budding trees, and an overall sense of renewal. Roasted artichokes and gently steamed baby vegetables served with luxurious cashew cream and crispy onion rings say, "Welcome, springtime" in a most delicious way. Note that the cashews must soak overnight before using—this makes them very light and creamy.

Cashew Cream
½ cup raw cashews
½ teaspoon sea salt
½ cup water

Vegetables
4 medium artichokes
2 tablespoons extra-virgin olive oil
1 tablespoon freshly squeezed lemon juice
Sea salt and freshly ground pepper
12 fresh asparagus spears, trimmed and cut into 1-inch pieces
1 cup baby carrots
1 cup fresh or frozen shelled fava beans, thawed if frozen
1 cup fresh or frozen green peas, thawed if frozen

Onion Rings
1 tablespoon Ener-G egg replacer
½ cup soy milk
½ cup fine yellow cornmeal
¼ cup arrowroot powder
Sea salt and freshly ground pepper
1 large yellow onion, sliced into ¼-inch rings
3 tablespoons safflower oil

2 tablespoons extra-virgin olive oil
2 shallots, thinly sliced
½ cup white wine
½ cup chopped fresh chives
Sea salt and freshly ground pepper
Microgreens or sprouts, for garnish

Serves 4

To make the Cashew Cream, the day before using, put the cashews in a bowl and add enough cold water to cover them. Cover and let soak overnight in the refrigerator.

Drain and rinse the cashews and put them in a blender. Add the salt and water and process until creamy, adding more water or salt if necessary.

Preheat the oven to 350°F.

To prepare the vegetables, trim and discard the stems and tough outer leaves of the artichokes. Halve the artichokes, remove the furry center, and put them in a large roasting pan, cut side up. Whisk together the olive oil and lemon juice, and season with salt and pepper. Drizzle over the artichokes and toss well to coat. Cover with foil and bake until tender, 20 to 30 minutes.

Leave the oven on. Put the asparagus, carrots, fava beans, and peas in a steamer basket and steam until just tender, 8 to 10 minutes. Drain and set aside.

Meanwhile, make the onion rings. Whisk together the egg replacer and soy milk in a shallow bowl. In another shallow bowl, stir together the cornmeal and arrowroot powder, and season with salt and pepper. Dip the onion slices into the soy milk, then the cornmeal mixture. Heat the safflower oil in a cast-iron skillet over medium-high heat. Gently place the rings in the oil and cook for 3 minutes on each side, adding more oil if needed. Drain on paper towels.

continued

Heat the 2 tablespoons of olive oil in a sauté pan over medium heat. Add the shallots and sauté until translucent, about 3 minutes. Add the white wine, decrease the heat, and simmer until the liquid reduces by half. Add the steamed vegetables, season with salt and pepper, and stir for 1 minute. Set the mixture aside. In the same pan, heat the Cashew Cream and chives over low heat, stirring occasionally, for about 5 minutes or until warm.

To serve, spoon 4 tablespoons of the cashew cream onto each of 4 plates. Divide the vegetable mixture among the plates. Stack 1 or 2 onion rings on top of the vegetables. Place 2 artichoke halves on top of the onion rings, then garnish with the microgreens to form a beautiful spring tower. Serve at once.

Avocado Salsa

This guacamole-type salsa, served with chips or on cucumber slices, makes a wonderful appetizer. It also makes a terrific topping for our Black Bean–Chipotle Burgers (page 95). Note: If you prefer a spicier salsa, use a whole jalapeño pepper.

3 ripe avocados
½ cup cherry or grape tomatoes, halved or quartered
2 tablespoons freshly squeezed lime juice
1 scallion, white and green parts, minced
½ jalapeño pepper, seeded and minced
½ teaspoon minced fresh oregano
½ teaspoon minced fresh thyme
½ teaspoon sea salt
Chips or cucumber slices, for serving

Makes about 3 cups

Halve the avocados. Carefully press the blade of a sharp knife into the pit, twist, and pull gently to remove. Cut ¼-inch slices horizontally and vertically into the flesh of the avocados to make medium-sized squares. Scoop out the flesh with a large spoon.

Combine the avocados, tomatoes, lime juice, scallion, jalapeño pepper, oregano, thyme, and salt in a bowl. Gently mix together, being careful not to break up the avocados.

If not serving immediately, cover and store in the refrigerator for up to 2 hours. Serve chilled or at room temperature, with the chips or cucumber slices alongside.

Zucchini Blossom Tempura

Tempura, a Japanese style of preparation in which food is batter-dipped and deep-fried, is an addictive way to prepare zucchini flowers, the golden blossoms that eventually give way to baby zucchini. Stuffed with tofu cheese, these springtime treats make wonderful appetizers or snacks to nibble on with cocktails. For a heartier presentation, serve them over a salad of tomatoes and artichoke hearts, drizzled with a balsamic reduction, and garnished with sprouts and microgreens, as shown in the photo. Note: If you're unfamiliar with egg replacer, see the Glossary (page 179) for more information and Resources (page 182) for sources.

Tofu Cheese
1 pound firm tofu
2 tablespoons freshly squeezed
    lemon juice
2 tablespoons nutritional yeast
1 tablespoon extra-virgin olive oil
1 teaspoon sea salt

Tempura Batter
¾ cup Ener-G egg replacer
¼ cup arrowroot powder
¼ cup unbleached all-purpose flour
1 teaspoon sea salt
¼ cup fine yellow cornmeal
2 cups soy milk

16 zucchini blossoms, stemmed and
    small leaves removed
2 cups safflower oil, for frying

Serves 4 to 6

To make the Tofu Cheese, put the tofu in a saucepan, add water to cover by 1 inch, and simmer for 20 minutes. Turn off the heat and let the tofu cool in the water. Drain the tofu and press with paper towels to remove excess water. Crumble the tofu into a food processor fitted with the metal blade. Add the lemon juice, nutritional yeast, olive oil, and salt and process until smooth.

To make the batter, put the egg replacer, arrowroot powder, flour, salt, and cornmeal in a bowl and stir together. Whisk in the soy milk until well combined.

Using a pastry bag or small spoon, stuff each squash blossom with the tofu mixture.

Heat the safflower oil in a deep cast-iron skillet over medium-high heat until hot but not smoking. Dip each blossom in the tempura batter and let the excess drip off, then deep-fry until golden and crispy, about 2 minutes. Drain on paper towels and serve at once.

Arancini with Roasted Plum Tomato Sauce

Arancini are small rice croquettes that are said to have originated in ancient Sicily. Our scrumptious vegan version is made with risotto balls stuffed with tempeh bacon and Daiya cheese. Daiya cheese, which is made from tapioca flour and is an excellent alternative for those allergic to soy and nuts, is available in cheddar or mozzarella flavors and can be purchased at natural food stores. This has become one of our signature appetizers. We also serve these bite-sized treats at parties and special events, and they always win raves from our guests.

¼ cup plus 1 teaspoon extra-virgin olive oil
2 tablespoons chopped shallot
½ teaspoon sea salt
1 cup Arborio rice
½ cup white wine
2 cups water
½ teaspoon chopped fresh flat-leaf parsley
½ cup shredded Daiya mozzarella cheese
¼ cup tempeh bacon, cooked, drained, and crumbled
1 cup dried bread crumbs or panko
2½ cups Roasted Plum Tomato Sauce (page 116), for dipping
Microgreens, for garnish

Serves 6 to 8; makes about 18 rice balls

Heat 1 teaspoon of the olive oil in a saucepan over medium heat. Add the shallot and salt and sauté for 1 minute. Add the rice and cook, stirring until coated, for 2 minutes. Add the wine and cook for 3 to 5 minutes, until it is absorbed. Add 1 cup of the water, decrease the heat, and simmer, stirring often, until most of the water is absorbed. Add the remaining 1 cup of water and continue to cook in the same way until the water is absorbed and the rice is al dente but not mushy, about 30 minutes altogether.

Remove from the heat and stir well. Stir in the parsley and ¼ cup of the cheese and let cool for 20 minutes.

Put the tempeh bacon and the remaining ¼ cup of cheese in a small bowl and stir well to combine.

Using your hands, a spoon, or an ice cream scoop, shape a bit of the rice mixture into a 1½-inch ball, then make an indentation in the center that extends halfway into the ball. Fill with about 1 teaspoon of the tempeh mixture, then roll to cover the filling. Repeat with the remaining ingredients to make about 18 rice balls. Roll the rice balls in the bread crumbs, shaking off any excess.

Heat the ¼ cup of olive oil in a sauté pan over medium heat. Fry the rice balls, turning often, until golden brown, 4 to 5 minutes. Serve with the tomato sauce on the side for dipping, or nestle the arancini in the sauce. Garnish with the microgreens and serve at once.

Smoked Paprika Hummus

We like to make hummus with dried chickpeas (which need to soak overnight), but if you're short on time canned chickpeas will do. In addition to the standard chickpeas, lemon juice, and tahini, we add a generous spoonful of smoked paprika to our hummus for a deep, rich flavor. We serve it with grilled paratha bread, olives, roasted garlic, and a drizzle of red pepper oil. After New York Times *food critic Frank Bruni visited our restaurant, he wrote about this dish, describing it as "one of the more enjoyable hummuses I've had in the city."*

1 cup dried chickpeas, or
    2 (15.5-ounce) cans chickpeas,
    drained and rinsed
2 large cloves garlic, minced
1 teaspoon freshly squeezed lemon
    juice
¼ teaspoon cayenne pepper
2 teaspoons smoked paprika, plus
    more for garnish
½ teaspoon sea salt
½ teaspoon freshly ground pepper
2 tablespoons finely chopped fresh
    flat-leaf parsley
⅓ cup extra-virgin olive oil, plus
    more for garnish
⅓ cup tahini
Optional garnishes: roasted red bell
    peppers, roasted garlic, lemon
    slices, olives, mint or parsley
    sprigs

Makes about 3 cups

If using dried chickpeas, put them in a saucepan or bowl and add cold water to cover by about 2 inches. Soak in the refrigerator for at least 6 hours or overnight. Drain and rinse.

Put the chickpeas in a saucepan and add cold water to cover by about 2 inches. Bring to a boil, decrease the heat, cover, and simmer until the chickpeas are tender, 50 to 60 minutes. Drain and let cool, reserving ¼ to ½ cup of the cooking water.

Combine the chickpeas, garlic, lemon juice, cayenne, paprika, salt, pepper, parsley, olive oil, and tahini in a bowl and stir to mix well. Transfer the mixture to a food processor fitted with the metal blade and process until well mixed. Add ¼ cup of the reserved cooking liquid (or water or vegetable stock if using canned chickpeas) and process until smooth and almost fluffy. Add more liquid if necessary. Scrape down the sides of the bowl once or twice. Transfer to a serving bowl and refrigerate for at least 1 hour. (The hummus can be made up to 3 days ahead and refrigerated. Return to room temperature before serving.)

To serve, drizzle a bit of olive oil over the hummus and sprinkle a bit of paprika. Serve with desired garnishes.

Cashew Cheese–Stuffed Yuca Cakes

Yuca, also known as cassava, is a starchy, potato-like root vegetable that is very high in vitamins A, B, and C, as well as calcium, phosphorus, potassium, and iron. In this dish we cook the yuca, form it into little cakes, and stuff them with creamy cashew cheese. The velvety centers of these tasty morsels add a rich texture that contrasts beautifully with the crispy outsides of the cakes. Note that the cashews must soak overnight before using.

Cashew Cheese
1 cup raw cashews
1 tablespoon extra-virgin olive oil
½ cup finely diced onions
½ cup finely diced leek
1 tablespoon freshly squeezed lemon
    juice
1½ teaspoons nutritional yeast
Pinch of sea salt

2 pounds yuca, peeled, cored, and
    cut into ½- to 1-inch chunks
2 teaspoons chopped fresh flat-leaf
    parsley
2 tablespoons extra-virgin olive oil
1 teaspoon sea salt
Tarragon Aioli (page 126), for
    accompaniment
1 cup Mint-Cilantro Chimichurri
    Sauce (page 120), for
    accompaniment
3 to 6 tablespoons extra-virgin olive
    oil or safflower oil, for frying

Serves 4 to 6

To make the Cashew Cheese, the day before serving, put the cashews in a bowl and add enough cold water to cover them. Cover and let soak overnight in the refrigerator.

Heat the oil in a sauté pan over medium heat. Add the onion and leek and sauté until softened, about 3 minutes.

Drain the cashews and transfer to a food processor fitted with the metal blade. Add the lemon juice, nutritional yeast, and salt and process until smooth, about 3 minutes. Add the onion and leek and process for another minute. Set aside.

Bring a large pot of water to a boil over high heat. Add the yuca and cook until very tender, 15 to 20 minutes. Drain and let cool a bit, then transfer to a large bowl.

Mash the yuca until smooth. Add the parsley, olive oil, and salt and mash again until smooth.

Using your hands or an ice cream scoop, form the yuca mixture into 2-inch balls. For each cake, make a deep indentation in the middle of a ball with your thumb and stuff with 1 tablespoon of the cashew mixture. Pinch the hole to close, then flatten into a cake with the palm of your hand. The cakes should measure about 2 inches in diameter and 1 inch thick.

Heat 3 tablespoons of the oil in a large nonstick sauté pan over medium heat. Fry the cakes until golden brown, about 3 minutes per side, adding more oil if necessary. Drain on paper towels.

To serve, place a cake in the center of a plate, top with a dollop of the aioli, and drizzle with the chimichurri sauce.

Spinach-Mushroom Pâté

This versatile and rich-tasting pâté is an all-time favorite appetizer at Candle 79. It's lovely to serve at a party with cocktails or a crisp, organic white wine. Spoon it onto crostini made with your favorite bread or onto crackers, or serve it alongside a crudité platter.

2 tablespoons extra-virgin olive oil
½ cup finely chopped shallots
5 whole portobello mushrooms,
    peeled and cut into small cubes
½ pound fresh spinach, chopped
2 cloves garlic, minced
½ teaspoon sea salt
⅛ teaspoon freshly ground pepper
¾ cup vegan mayonnaise
12 crostini

Makes about 2 cups, or a dozen crostini

Heat 1 tablespoon of the olive oil in a sauté pan over medium heat. Add the shallots and mushrooms and sauté until softened, 5 to 7 minutes. Drain any excess liquid, transfer to a bowl, and let cool.

Wipe out the sauté pan and heat the remaining tablespoon of olive oil over medium heat. Add the spinach, garlic, salt, and pepper and cook until the spinach is wilted, 3 to 5 minutes. Set aside to cool.

Put the mushroom and spinach mixtures in a food processor fitted with the metal blade and process until smooth, about 3 minutes. Transfer to a bowl and stir in the mayonnaise. Taste and adjust the seasonings if necessary. Spoon onto the crostini and serve warm, chilled, or at room temperature.

Seitan Cakes

We serve these very tasty fried cakes as an appetizer with a hearty dollop of Cashew Crème Fraîche (page 125), julienned apple or Granny Smith Coleslaw (page 101), and microgreens, as shown here. They are full of flavor and texture, and they're also a lot of fun to experiment with—you can add lemon, thyme, stone-ground mustard, or mustard powder to the mix or substitute panko for the bread crumbs.

2 tablespoons Ener-G egg replacer
¼ cup warm water
1 pound seitan, coarsely chopped
¼ cup finely diced leek, white and pale green parts
¼ cup finely diced shallots
½ teaspoon finely chopped garlic
¼ cup finely diced celery
2 tablespoons unbleached all-purpose flour
1 teaspoon smoked paprika
½ teaspoon Old Bay Seasoning
1 teaspoon sea salt
¼ teaspoon freshly ground pepper
½ cup bread crumbs
3 to 6 tablespoons extra-virgin olive oil, for frying

Serves 4 to 6

Whisk the egg replacer and water together. Put the mixture in a large bowl. Add the seitan, leek, shallots, garlic, celery, flour, paprika, Old Bay Seasoning, salt, and pepper and mix with your hands for 2 minutes. Add up to ¼ cup of the bread crumbs to absorb moisture and hold the cakes together.

Form into small cakes about 2½ inches in diameter and ½ inch thick, pressing firmly. Put the remaining bread crumbs in a shallow bowl or on a plate and dredge the cakes in the crumbs to coat. Let the cakes sit for 10 minutes.

Heat 3 tablespoons of the oil in a large nonstick sauté pan over medium heat. Fry the cakes until golden brown, about 3 minutes per side, adding more oil if necessary. Drain on paper towels. Alternatively, you can bake the cakes. Preheat the oven to 350°F. Put the cakes on a baking sheet and brush with olive oil. Bake until golden brown, about 10 minutes. Serve warm.

Ginger-Seitan Dumplings

These delicious little bundles of heaven are packed with flavor. Shiitake mushrooms, ginger, and scallions add just the right zip to the filling. These are great to serve with bok choy for a cocktail party or as a first course. Note: Vegan wonton wrappers are available at natural food stores and specialty markets (see Resources, page 182).

1 pound seitan
1 cup shiitake mushrooms, stemmed
    and chopped
1 tablespoon extra-virgin olive oil
1 tablespoon toasted sesame oil
1 cup finely chopped scallions, white
    and green parts
2 tablespoons finely chopped fresh
    ginger
2 tablespoons tamari
2 tablespoons freshly squeezed
    lemon juice
1 package of vegan wonton wrappers
    (at least 40 count)
Safflower oil, for frying
1¼ cups Ginger-Soy Dipping Sauce
    (page 115), for accompaniment

Serves 8 to 10; makes about 40 dumplings

Drain the seitan and squeeze out the excess liquid. Put the seitan in a food processor fitted with the metal blade and process for 2 minutes, until thoroughly ground. Add the shiitake mushrooms and process for another minute.

Heat the olive oil and sesame oil in a sauté pan over medium heat. Add the scallions, ginger, tamari, and lemon juice and sauté for 2 minutes. Add the seitan mixture and cook for 10 minutes, stirring occasionally. Remove from the heat and let cool for 1 hour. Drain the mixture in a fine-mesh sieve to remove any excess liquid.

Spoon about 1 tablespoon of the mixture onto a wonton wrapper. Using a pastry brush, dab some water on the corners of the wonton wrap. Pull up all four corners and pinch the four edges tightly shut. Twist the top point to complete the seal. Repeat until all the filling and about 40 wrappers are used.

Heat ½ inch of safflower oil in a large sauté pan over medium heat and fry the dumplings, turning often, until golden brown, about 3 minutes, working in batches if need be. The dumplings can also be steamed in a mesh basket.

Serve warm with the dipping sauce alongside.

Soups

There's something about soups that nourishes the body and soul. They can be served as an appetizer or a meal in a bowl, as an intimate dinner or a feast for a crowd. We make them year-round and use the freshest seasonal ingredients available. We prefer subtly seasoning soups with sesame oil, miso, and tamari and infusing them with fresh herbs for deep, satisfying flavor. Our founder, Bart Potenza, always says, "There is no finer meal than a bowl of soup and a hunk of bread." We think that you'll agree.

Live Avocado-Cucumber Soup

Many people believe that cooking diminishes the amount of vitamins, minerals, and enzymes in food and seek out "live" (uncooked or raw) dishes like this summer soup. One of Candle 79's most requested seasonal dishes, this rich and creamy blend of avocados, garden-fresh cucumbers, cilantro, and mint is scrumptious and satisfying. For warm-weather parties and barbecues, we often serve mini portions in shot glasses.

2 ripe avocados, halved, pitted, peeled, and diced
4 cucumbers, peeled, seeded, and chopped
½ jalapeño pepper, seeded and finely diced
½ cup chopped fresh cilantro, plus cilantro sprigs for garnish
2 tablespoons fresh lime juice
2 tablespoons fresh lemon juice
½ cup water
1 teaspoon sea salt
1 julienned radish, for garnish
½ red bell pepper, seeded and cut into thin strips, for garnish
½ cup fresh corn kernels, for garnish

Serves 4 to 6

Put the avocados, cucumbers, jalapeño pepper, cilantro, lime juice, lemon juice, water, and salt in a blender and process until smooth. Taste and adjust the seasonings if necessary. Cover and chill in the refrigerator for at least 1 hour.

To serve, ladle the soup into bowls and garnish each serving with the radish, bell pepper, corn, and a cliantro sprig.

Farmers' Market Gazpacho

We love to make runs downtown to the Union Square Farmers' Market all year round to check out the fabulous local produce. There is no better time to go than summer when everything is at its ripest peak. We look for the juiciest tomatoes we can find to make this refreshing gazpacho. There are no hard-and-fast rules in making this recipe—you can adjust the tomato juice and the amounts and types of vegetables to your liking. Note that the soup is best chilled overnight in the refrigerator.

3 pounds ripe tomatoes, coarsely
    chopped
1 to 2 cups tomato juice
1 teaspoon sea salt
½ cup finely diced red bell pepper
½ cup finely diced celery
½ cup finely diced red onion
½ cup peeled, seeded, and diced
    cucumber
10 fresh basil leaves, finely chopped,
    plus whole basil leaves for
    garnish

Serves 4 to 6

Put the tomatoes, tomato juice, and salt in a blender and process until very smooth. Transfer to a large bowl or container.

Add the bell pepper, celery, onion, cucumbers, and chopped basil to the soup and stir well. Cover, and chill in the refrigerator for at least 8 hours or overnight. Taste and adjust the seasonings if necessary.

To serve, ladle the soup into bowls and garnish with the whole basil leaves.

Tortilla Soup

This festive soup has a deep and rich flavor that comes from roasting the tomatoes and bell peppers with pasilla chiles—very dark, dried chiles that have a deep, almost chocolate-like flavor. We also add a sprig of epazote, a flavorful leafy green herb, to add hints of citrus and mint to the soup. If you can't find epazote, substitute 2 teaspoons of finely chopped fresh cilantro. Pasilla chiles and epazote are available at Latin markets, specialty grocery stores, and online. We like to serve this soup as a starter with Stuffed Poblano Peppers (page 58) or Chile-Grilled Tofu (page 76).

1 cup safflower oil
6 (6-inch) corn tortillas, cut into
    ¼-inch strips
1 pound tomatoes, halved
1 red bell pepper, seeded and
    quartered
2 dried pasilla chiles
½ cup chopped white onion
1 clove garlic, chopped
Pinch of sea salt
2 tablespoons grapeseed oil
1 cup drained seitan pieces
5 cups vegetable stock
1 sprig epazote
Scallions, green parts only, cut into
    thin strips, for garnish

Serves 6

Preheat the oven to 350°F.

In a deep cast-iron skillet, heat the safflower oil over medium-high heat until hot but not smoking. Add the tortilla strips and fry until crisp and golden brown, 3 to 5 minutes. Remove with a slotted spoon and drain on paper towels.

Put the tomato halves, cut side up, on a rimmed baking sheet and roast for 10 minutes. Let cool, then peel. Put the bell peppers on another rimmed baking sheet and roast until tender, 30 to 40 minutes. Let cool, then coarsely chop. Put the pasilla chiles on a small baking sheet and roast for 3 minutes. Let the chiles cool, then crumble and set aside.

Put the roasted tomatoes, onion, garlic, and salt in a blender and process until smooth.

In a soup pot, heat the grapeseed oil over medium heat. Add the seitan and the tomato mixture and cook, stirring occasionally, for 5 minutes. Stir in the stock and roasted bell pepper and cook for 10 minutes. Stir in the crumbled pasilla chiles and epazote sprig and cook for 10 minutes. Taste and adjust the seasonings if necessary.

To serve, ladle the soup into bowls, garnish each serving with the tortilla strips and scallions, and serve at once.

Jerusalem Artichoke Soup with Crispy Sage Leaves

Knobby, brown-skinned Jerusalem artichokes are not truly artichokes, but a variety of sunflower (they get their name from girasole, *Italian for sunflower). They are also sold as sunchokes. Their hearty, earthy taste works beautifully in soup, enhanced in this recipe with a garnish of sautéed fresh sage leaves.*

¼ cup extra-virgin olive oil
1 leek, white and pale green parts,
    rinsed and finely chopped
½ cup finely chopped white onion
2 pounds Jerusalem artichokes,
    peeled and rinsed
5 cups water or vegetable stock
1 teaspoon sea salt

Crispy Sage Leaves
1 tablespoon extra-virgin olive oil
8 to 12 fresh sage leaves

Serves 4 to 6

Heat the olive oil in a soup pot over medium heat. Add the leek and onion and sauté until softened, about 5 minutes. Add the Jerusalem artichokes, water, and salt and bring to a boil. Decrease the heat, cover, and simmer until the artichokes are tender, about 30 minutes.

Remove from the heat and let cool. Transfer the mixture to a blender and process until smooth. Taste and adjust the seasonings if necessary. Gently reheat before serving.

To crisp the sage leaves, heat the olive oil in a small sauté pan over medium heat. Add the sage leaves and sauté until just crisp, about 2 minutes. Drain on paper towels. Garnish each serving with a couple of the sage leaves.

Herbed Potato-Leek Soup

Fresh leeks have a sweet and delicate flavor that is subtler than onions. We like to use them in all types of soups, sauces, and stews, and they also taste great simply sautéed in olive oil. Here, the leeks are cooked and pureed with potatoes and herbs to create a creamy, earthy soup.

6 cups vegetable stock or water
1½ pounds Yukon gold potatoes, peeled and coarsely chopped
2 leeks, white and pale green parts, rinsed and finely chopped
1 teaspoon chopped fresh chives
1 teaspoon chopped fresh oregano
1 teaspoon chopped fresh thyme
1 teaspoon chopped fresh flat-leaf parsley
2 teaspoons sea salt
Pinch of freshly ground pepper
Dill sprigs, for garnish

Serves 4 to 6

Put the stock, potatoes, and leeks in a soup pot and bring to a boil. Add the chives, oregano, thyme, parsley, salt, and pepper. Decrease the heat and simmer, uncovered, until the vegetables are very tender, about 30 minutes. Remove from the heat and set aside to cool.

Transfer the soup to a blender and process until smooth (in batches if necessary). Return the soup to the pot and gently reheat. Taste and adjust the seasonings if necessary, garnish with the dill sprigs, and serve at once.

Black Bean and Roasted Poblano Soup

Rich and satisfying, this soup blends roasted red bell peppers and poblano peppers with earthy black beans infused with smoky chipotle powder. It's the perfect choice to make and eat on a chilly winter's night. Note that the dried beans must soak for at least 6 hours.

1 cup dried black beans, rinsed and picked over, or 2 (15.5-ounce) cans black beans, drained and rinsed
1 red bell pepper
1 poblano pepper
3 tablespoons extra-virgin olive oil
1 large leek, white and pale green parts, rinsed and finely chopped
3 cloves garlic, finely chopped
½ cup chopped red onion
8 cups vegetable stock or water, or as needed
2 ripe tomatoes, finely chopped
⅛ teaspoon chipotle chile powder
Sea salt and freshly ground pepper
Cashew Crème Fraîche (page 125), for garnish
2 tablespoons finely chopped fresh cilantro, for garnish

Serves 4 to 6

If using dried beans, put them in a saucepan or bowl and add cold water to cover by about 2 inches. Soak for at least 6 hours or overnight in the refrigerator. Drain and rinse.

Brush the peppers with olive oil. With a long fork or tongs, cook the peppers over an open flame, turning often, until the skin is charred all over, about 5 minutes per side. Put the peppers in a large bowl. Cover with plastic wrap and let cool. When cool enough to handle, peel off the skins, remove the seeds, and chop them.

Heat the remaining 2 tablespoons of olive oil in a soup pot over medium heat. Add the leek, garlic, and onion and sauté until softened, about 5 minutes. Add the beans and stock (use only 4 cups stock if using canned beans). Stir well, decrease the heat, and simmer, uncovered, for about 1 hour or until the beans are tender, adding more liquid if needed.

Stir in the roasted peppers, tomatoes, and chipotle powder, season with salt and pepper, and simmer for 10 minutes. Taste and adjust the seasonings if necessary. Garnish with the Cashew Crème Fraîche and cilantro and serve warm.

Butternut Squash–Chestnut Soup with Caramelized Pears

We take full advantage of the bountiful squash harvest every autumn and make a number of hearty dishes with it. This smooth, creamy soup, simmered with a cheesecloth pouch filled with autumnal spices and topped with fragrant caramelized pears, is one of our seasonal favorites. It's a perfect addition to any fall menu and is also a fantastic starter for Thanksgiving dinner.

1 cinnamon stick
1 whole nutmeg, halved
1 stalk lemongrass, chopped
2 cardamom pods
1 (1-inch) piece of fresh ginger, peeled and chopped
2 dried chipotle chiles
¼ cup extra-virgin olive oil
1 large leek, white and pale green parts, rinsed and finely chopped
3 pounds butternut squash, peeled and cut into 1-inch dice
1 cup drained canned or jarred chestnuts, chopped
2 tablespoons chopped fresh sage
8 cups water

Balsamic-Caramelized Pears
1 tablespoon grapeseed or safflower oil
2 ripe pears, peeled, cored, and diced
1 tablespoon pure maple syrup
1 teaspoon ground cinnamon
1 teaspoon balsamic vinegar
Sea salt and freshly ground pepper

2 to 3 tablespoons pure maple syrup
Sea salt

Serves 6 to 8

Put the cinnamon stick, nutmeg, lemongrass, cardamom pods, ginger, and chipotle peppers in cheesecloth. Knot securely or tie with string and set aside.

Heat the olive oil in a soup pot over medium heat. Add the leek and sauté until softened, about 10 minutes. Add the squash, chestnuts, sage, cheesecloth pouch, and water. The water should cover the squash by about 2 inches. Bring to a boil, decrease the heat, cover, and simmer until the squash is tender and falls apart, 30 to 45 minutes. Remove from the heat and let cool.

To make the caramelized pears, heat the oil in a large sauté pan over high heat. Add the pears and sauté for 5 minutes. Decrease the heat to medium and stir in the maple syrup, cinnamon, vinegar, and salt and pepper to taste. Continue to cook for 10 to 15 minutes, until the pears are soft and the liquid becomes syrupy and coats the pears. Set aside to cool.

To finish the soup, remove the cheesecloth pouch and discard. Add the maple syrup and salt to taste. Transfer the soup to a blender and process until smooth, or process the soup in the pot with an immersion blender. If the soup seems too thick, add a bit more water.

To serve, gently reheat the soup, taste, and adjust the seasonings if necessary. Ladle into soup bowls, garnish with the caramelized pears, and serve warm.

Salads

Salads are a mainstay of the Candle 79 menu and a staple of every vegan diet. They are healthful, easy to prepare, and add great flavor, texture, and beauty to every meal. We serve all types of salads year-round as both starters and main courses, combining vibrant greens, vegetables, fruits, and grains with flavorful vinaigrettes and dressings.

All good cooks know that buying what's in season is key in preparing great-tasting food. This is especially true with salads, as freshness is the heart and soul of a perfect salad. Explore your local farmers' markets and produce sections, take advantage of each season's bounty of ingredients, and you can't go wrong.

Heirloom Tomato Salad with Macadamia Cheese and Crispy Capers

This combination of heirloom tomatoes, creamy nut cheese, and briny, crispy capers is divine. The macadamia nuts need to soak overnight, so plan accordingly. If you like, you can make the balsamic reduction up to a week ahead and store it in a covered glass container in a cool, dark place. It serves as an excellent addition to many different salads—or even as a drizzle over berries.

Macadamia Cheese
2 cups macadamia nuts
1 teaspoon sea salt
2 tablespoons nutritional yeast
1 tablespoon freshly squeezed lemon
    juice

1 cup balsamic vinegar
2 tablespoons sugar

Crispy Capers
½ cup capers, drained
⅓ cup grapeseed oil

½ pound baby arugula
2 pounds heirloom tomatoes, cut
    into wedges
Cherry tomatoes, for garnish
Sprouts or microgreens, for garnish
Extra-virgin olive oil, for drizzling
    (optional)
Freshly ground pepper (optional)

Serves 4 to 6

To make the Macadamia Cheese, the day before serving, put the macadamia nuts in a bowl and add enough cold water to cover them. Cover and let soak overnight in the refrigerator.

Drain the nuts and transfer to a food processor fitted with the metal blade. Add the salt, nutritional yeast, and lemon juice and process until very smooth. Set aside.

Put the balsamic vinegar and sugar in a saucepan over medium heat and simmer until reduced to ¼ cup, 20 to 25 minutes. Set aside.

To prepare the capers, let them dry on paper towels for 10 minutes. Heat the oil in a sauté pan over medium-high heat. Add the capers and decrease the heat to medium-low. Cook the capers, stirring often, until crispy, 5 to 8 minutes. Remove with a slotted spoon and transfer to paper towels to drain.

To assemble the salad, place some of the arugula in the center of each salad plate. Arrange the tomato wedges atop the arugula, tuck in a few cherry tomatoes, then top with sprouts. Put a dollop of the cheese atop the sprouts. Sprinkle the capers over the cheese, then garnish with a drizzle of olive oil and a dusting of pepper if desired. Drizzle the balsamic reduction on the plate and serve at once.

Butterhead Lettuce, Cauliflower, and Red Bell Pepper Salad

Made with roasted Mediterranean vegetables and chickpeas and drizzled with a bright-tasting sun-dried tomato vinaigrette, this salad can be served as an appetizer or a main dish. Look for big, loose heads of butterhead lettuce at the farmers' market in late spring through summer. Popular varieties of this lettuce include Boston, Bibb, and Buttercrunch.

1 cup dried chickpeas, or
    2 (15.5-ounce) cans chickpeas,
    drained and rinsed
2 red bell peppers
3 tablespoons extra-virgin olive oil
1 head cauliflower (about
    2 pounds), trimmed and cut into
    florets
2 tablespoons water
Sea salt and freshly ground pepper

Vinaigrette
¼ cup balsamic vinegar
¼ cup finely chopped shallots
½ teaspoon sugar
¼ cup oil-packed or rehydrated
    sun-dried tomatoes, drained and
    finely diced
½ teaspoon sea salt
1 teaspoon freshly ground pepper
½ cup extra-virgin olive oil

½ pound butterhead lettuce, torn
    into bite-sized pieces
½ cup shelled pistachios, for garnish

Serves 6

If using dried chickpeas, put them in a saucepan or bowl and add cold water to cover by about 2 inches. Cover and soak the beans for at least 6 to 8 hours or overnight in the refrigerator. Drain and rinse.

Put the chickpeas in a saucepan and add cold water to cover by about 2 inches. Bring to a boil, decrease the heat, cover, and simmer until the chickpeas are tender, 50 to 60 minutes. Drain and let cool.

Preheat the oven to 350°F.

Put the peppers on a rimmed baking sheet and drizzle with 1 tablespoon of the olive oil. Roast until tender, 20 to 30 minutes. Transfer to a bowl, cover with plastic wrap, and let cool. Peel, stem, and seed the peppers and cut into thin slices.

Meanwhile, put the cauliflower, the remaining 2 tablespoons of olive oil, and the water in a large bowl, season with salt and pepper, and toss together. Transfer to a baking pan, cover with aluminum foil, and roast until just tender, 15 to 20 minutes. Set aside to cool.

To make the vinaigrette, whisk together the vinegar, shallots, sugar, sun-dried tomatoes, salt, and pepper until the sugar is dissolved. Slowly whisk in the extra-virgin olive oil until well combined.

Put the peppers, cauliflower, chickpeas, and lettuce in a large salad bowl. Pour the vinaigrette over the salad and toss well to mix.

Divide the salad among salad plates, garnish with the pistachios, and serve.

Watercress, Jicama, and Corn Salad with Jalapeño Dressing

We like to use fresh jicama in a number of our dishes. Crisp, refreshing, and slightly sweet, it's also fat free and high in vitamin C. In this salad, we toss it together with roasted red bell peppers, fresh corn, watercress, and a piquant jalapeño dressing for a sumptuous blend of Southwestern flavors. Sliced mango can serve as a good substitute for jicama. Note: To toast pumpkin seeds, vigorously shake and stir them in a pan over medium heat until they start to pop.

3 ears of fresh corn, husked
2 bunches watercress, stemmed
1 jicama, peeled and cut into 1-inch julienne
2 red bell peppers, seeded and cut into 1-inch julienne

Jalapeño Dressing
2 jalapeño peppers, seeded and chopped
½ cup chopped fresh cilantro
6 scallions, white and green parts, minced
1 teaspoon sea salt
2 tablespoons freshly squeezed lemon juice
½ cup grapeseed oil
⅓ cup water

½ cup toasted pumpkin seeds, for garnish

Serves 6

Bring a large pot of water to a boil. Add the corn and cook until tender, about 5 minutes. Let cool, then cut the kernels off the cobs. Put the corn, watercress, jicama, and bell peppers in a large bowl and toss together.

To make the dressing, put the jalapeño peppers, cilantro, scallions, salt, lemon juice, oil, and water in a blender and process until smooth.

Gradually add the dressing to the watercress mixture and toss well to coat. Divide the salad among salad plates, garnish with the pumpkin seeds, and serve.

Wild Mushroom and Cipollini Salad with Fresh Horseradish Dressing

Roasted and caramelized cipollini and sautéed wild mushrooms are an unbeatable combination, and both are at their seasonal best in autumn. Cipollini are sometimes called wild onions but are really the bulbs of grape hyacinth. Here we combine them with a fantastic dressing that is packed with shallots and spicy fresh horseradish for an unforgettable fall salad.

1 pound cipollini, peeled and sliced crosswise
4 tablespoons extra-virgin olive oil
Sea salt and freshly ground pepper
1 pound oyster mushrooms, sliced
½ pound portobello mushrooms

Horseradish Dressing
½ cup plus 1 teaspoon extra-virgin olive oil
½ cup sliced shallots
½ cup trimmed, peeled, and diced fresh horseradish
½ pound silken tofu
⅓ cup white wine vinegar
1 teaspoon sea salt

½ pound baby arugula
2 cups grape tomatoes or cherry tomatoes, halved

Serves 6

Preheat the oven 350°F.

Put the cipollini on a rimmed baking sheet and drizzle with 1 tablespoon of the olive oil. Season with salt and pepper, and roast until tender, 20 to 30 minutes.

In a large sauté pan, heat the remaining 3 tablespoons of olive oil over medium heat for 1 minute. Add the mushrooms and sauté until they are browned and give up all of their liquid, about 8 minutes.

To make the dressing, heat the 1 teaspoon of olive oil in a sauté pan over medium heat. Add the shallots and sauté until softened, 3 to 5 minutes. Transfer to a blender. Add the horseradish, tofu, vinegar, salt, and the ½ cup of olive oil and process until smooth.

In a large bowl, toss the arugula and tomatoes together with half of the dressing. Divide the arugula mixture evenly among salad plates, placing it to one side of the plate. Spoon the remaining dressing onto the plates, making two small pools of dressing on each plate. Divide the mushrooms and cipollini among the plates, placing them atop the pools of dressing. Serve at once.

Kale, Vegetable, and Spelt Berry Salad with Chive Vinaigrette

Although it is often thought of as a green, kale is actually a form of cabbage—and a highly nutritious one. This salad is a delectable way to get more of this dark, leafy green into your diet. The delicious combination of quickly sautéed kale, roasted turnips, green beans, avocados, and sprightly chive vinaigrette is a meal in itself—and our customers often order it as a main course. To make this salad gluten free, substitute quinoa for spelt berries.

1 cup spelt berries

3 cups water

4 teaspoons extra-virgin olive oil

Sea salt and freshly ground pepper

1½ pounds baby turnips, peeled and quartered

½ pound green beans, trimmed

1 pound kale, stemmed and chopped

2 avocados, halved, pitted, peeled, and sliced

½ red onion, thinly sliced

Pinch of freshly ground pepper

Chive Vinaigrette

½ cup plus 1 tablespoon grapeseed oil

½ cup finely chopped shallots

2 cloves garlic, chopped

½ cup chopped fresh chives

¼ cup white wine vinegar

½ cup water

½ teaspoon sea salt

¼ teaspoon freshly ground pepper

Sunflower seeds, for garnish

Serves 6 to 8

Put the spelt berries in a bowl and add cold water to cover. Cover and soak overnight in the refrigerator. Drain and rinse.

Put the spelt berries in a saucepan. Add the water and 1 teaspoon of the olive oil, and season with salt and pepper. Bring to a boil, then decrease the heat and simmer, partially covered, until tender, 50 to 60 minutes. Set aside to cool.

Preheat the oven to 350°F.

Put the turnips on a rimmed baking sheet, drizzle with 1 teaspoon of the olive oil, season with salt and pepper, and toss to coat. Roast until tender, about 30 minutes.

Bring a pot of salted water to a boil. Add the green beans and cook until just tender, about 3 minutes. Drain immediately, rinse with cold water, and set aside.

In a bowl, toss the kale with the 2 remaining teaspoons of olive oil and season with salt and pepper. Transfer to a large sauté pan and cook over medium-high heat until it wilts and turns dark green, about 1 to 2 minutes. Set aside to cool, then transfer to a large bowl. Add the spelt berries, turnips, green beans, avocados, red onion, and pepper.

To make the dressing, heat the 1 tablespoon of grapeseed oil in a sauté pan over medium heat. Add the shallots and garlic and sauté until softened, 3 to 5 minutes. Transfer to a blender. Add the chives, vinegar, water, salt, and pepper and process until smooth.

Drizzle some of the vinaigrette over the vegetables and toss well. Divide among salad plates, drizzle with additional vinaigrette, garnish with the sunflower seeds, and serve.

Stuffed Avocado with Quinoa Pilaf and Chipotle-Avocado Dressing

This hearty, healthy salad can be served as a starter or a main course. Look for perfectly ripe avocados—they taste terrific stuffed with nutty quinoa and vegetables and drizzled with this smoky, mildly spicy avocado dressing.

Chipotle-Avocado Dressing

4 tablespoons extra-virgin olive oil
¼ cup chopped shallots
½ avocado, pitted, peeled,
    and diced
½ cup chopped fresh cilantro
2 cloves garlic, chopped
¼ teaspoon chipotle chile powder
2 guajillo chiles, chopped
3 tablespoons white wine vinegar
1 cup water
1 teaspoon sea salt

4 cups Quinoa-Vegetable Pilaf
    (page 107)
½ pound mixed fresh greens
4 avocados, halved, pitted, and
    peeled
4 radishes, thinly sliced, for garnish
¼ cup hemp seeds

Serves 8 as a starter, or 4 as an entrée

To make the dressing, heat 1 tablespoon of the olive oil in a sauté pan. Add the shallots and sauté until softened, about 3 minutes. Let cool, then transfer to a blender. Add the avocado, cilantro, garlic, chipotle powder, chiles, vinegar, water, salt, and the remaining 3 tablespoons of oil and process until smooth.

To assemble the salad, add half of the dressing to the quinoa and toss together. Arrange the greens on individual salad plates and top with 1 or 2 avocado halves each. Spoon the quinoa into the avocados and drizzle each serving with more of the dressing. Garnish with the radish slices, sprinkle with the hemp seeds, and serve.

Seaweed Salad with Ginger-Sesame Dressing

We serve this refreshing salad as a side to a variety of tofu and seitan dishes. It has converted our diners into seaweed lovers! We recommend arame or hijiki (or a mixture of both), which can be found at natural food stores and Asian markets. Note: To toast sesame seeds, vigorously shake and stir them in a pan over medium heat until they start to pop.

2 to 3 cups dried seaweed

Ginger-Sesame Dressing
2 tablespoons tamari
2 tablespoons water
1 tablespoon umeboshi vinegar
1 tablespoon brown rice vinegar
1½ teaspoons toasted sesame oil
1 teaspoon agave nectar
1½ teaspoons grated fresh ginger
1 teaspoon chopped garlic
½ teaspoon chopped scallions,
    white and green parts
½ teaspoon chopped fresh cilantro
Pinch of red pepper flakes
¼ cup grapeseed oil

1 carrot, cut into 1-inch julienne
4 radishes, peeled and cut into
    1-inch julienne
1 tablespoon toasted sesame seeds
½ pound mixed baby greens or baby
    arugula

Serves 4 to 6

Put the seaweed in a large bowl, cover with 4 cups of cold water and let soak until softened, 10 to 15 minutes. Drain, rinse with cold water, and let stand for 15 minutes.

To make the dressing, in a bowl whisk together the tamari, water, umeboshi vinegar, brown rice vinegar, sesame oil, agave nectar, ginger, garlic, scallions, cilantro, red pepper flakes, and grapeseed oil until well mixed.

To assemble the salad, add the carrot and radishes to the seaweed and toss together. Add the dressing and toss again. Sprinkle with the sesame seeds and serve chilled or at room temperature over the baby greens.

Beet, Fennel, and Fig Salad with Cranberry-Sage Dressing

This gorgeous early autumn salad is full of vibrant color and earthy flavor. Fresh figs have a fairly short growing season in the northeast, so we try to take full advantage of these iron- and fiber-rich beauties when they're available. They combine very well with every component of this salad. If you cannot find fresh cranberries, frozen ones will work just as well.

Cranberry-Sage Dressing
4 tablespoons extra-virgin olive oil
½ cup finely chopped shallots
1 cup fresh or frozen cranberries,
    thawed if frozen
¼ cup balsamic vinegar
1 teaspoon chopped fresh rosemary
    leaves
1 fresh sage leaf, chopped
⅓ cup water
1 tablespoon maple syrup
½ teaspoon sea salt

1 pound fresh beets
1 fennel bulb, trimmed and halved
Extra-virgin olive oil, for drizzling
Sea salt and freshly ground pepper
½ cup pecans
½ pound baby arugula
1 pear, cored and thinly sliced
    (optional)
6 fresh figs, cut into wedges

Serves 6

To make the dressing, heat 2 tablespoons of the olive oil in a large sauté pan over medium heat. Add the shallots and sauté until softened, about 5 minutes. Add the cranberries and cook, stirring, until they are softened and begin to pop, about 5 minutes. Set aside to cool, then transfer to a blender. Add the vinegar, rosemary, sage, water, maple syrup, salt, and the remaining 2 tablespoons olive oil and process until smooth.

Preheat oven to 350°F.

Wrap the beets in aluminum foil and put them on a baking sheet. Put the fennel on a separate baking sheet, cut side up, drizzle with olive oil, and season with salt and pepper. Put the beets and fennel in the oven and roast until fork-tender, about 30 minutes for the fennel, and 50 to 60 minutes for the beets. When cool enough to handle, peel the beets and cut into thin slices, and cut the fennel into very thin slices.

Meanwhile, spread the pecans on a baking sheet and bake until lightly toasted, about 5 to 8 minutes.

Put the arugula in a large bowl, add the beets, fennel, pecans, and optional pear, and gently toss together. Drizzle with the dressing and scatter the figs over the salad. Alternatively, divide the arugula evenly among salad plates, placing it to one side of the plate. Drizzle with the dressing and scatter the pecans on top. Arrange the beets, fennel, figs, and optional pear alongside the arugula and serve at once.

Blood Orange–Fennel Salad

The licorice flavor of fennel blends beautifully with sweet and tangy blood oranges in this simple, elegant salad. Be sure to slice the fennel as thinly as possible, using a mandoline or a very sharp knife. This sprightly, slightly acidic salad pairs beautifully with the earthy, nutty flavors of our Tempeh Cakes (page 80).

6 blood oranges, peeled and
    segmented
2 navel oranges, peeled and
    segmented
1 fennel bulb, trimmed and thinly
    sliced, fronds reserved and
    chopped for garnish
1 teaspoon chopped fresh flat-leaf
    parsley
2 tablespoons extra-virgin olive oil
¼ teaspoon salt
Pinch of freshly ground pepper
½ pound arugula, stemmed

Serves 4 to 6

Put the oranges, fennel, and parsley in a large bowl.

Whisk the olive oil together with the salt and pepper and pour over the orange mixture. Toss gently to coat.

Arrange the arugula on salad plates, top with the orange mixture, garnish with the reserved fennel fronds, and serve.

Mediterranean Salad with Kalamata Olive Vinaigrette

This savory salad takes full advantage of late summer grape tomatoes and cucumbers as well as early autumn fingerling potatoes. The vinaigrette, made with shiny black kalamata olives and a mélange of garden-fresh herbs, is so good that we also like to spoon it over greens, roasted vegetables, and grains.

½ pound fingerling potatoes, halved
    or quartered lengthwise
1 tablespoon extra-virgin olive oil
Sea salt and freshly ground pepper
2 cups grape tomatoes or cherry
    tomatoes, halved
1 cucumber, peeled, seeded, and
    thinly sliced
1 small red onion, thinly sliced
½ pound baby arugula

Vinaigrette
1 tablespoon stone-ground mustard
¼ cup white wine vinegar
1 tablespoon finely diced shallot
½ cup finely diced pitted kalamata
    olives
½ cup extra-virgin olive oil
1 teaspoon chopped fresh oregano
1 teaspoon chopped fresh thyme
1 tablespoon chopped fresh flat-leaf
    parsley
Freshly ground pepper

Serves 4 to 6

Preheat the oven to 350°F.

In a bowl, toss the potatoes with the olive oil and season with salt and pepper. Arrange in a single layer on a rimmed baking sheet and roast until tender and lightly browned, about 30 minutes. Let cool, then transfer to a large bowl. Add the tomatoes, cucumber, onion, and arugula and toss together.

To make the dressing, whisk all of the ingredients together in a small bowl.

Arrange the vegetable mixture on salad plates, drizzle with the vinaigrette, and serve.

Entrées

The entrées that we serve at Candle 79 prove that the main event need not always be based on meat or seafood. Our customers—vegans, vegetarians, and omnivores alike—are always amazed at how satisfying and varied our food is. Dishes based on the holy trinity of tofu, tempeh, and seitan make up most of our main dishes, but we also offer inventive, scrumptious entrées made with farm-fresh organic vegetables, house-made pastas, and a wide variety of grains and beans.

We have re-created our favorite dishes from the seasonal restaurant menu for the home cook (along with suggestions for delicious side dishes and sauces to serve with them in the next chapter). This is home cooking at its creative best, and we hope you will want to prepare these dishes for family and friends, and for yourself, again and again.

We've also included recommended wine pairings for each dish. While the classic rules of wine pairing often correspond to meat-based cuisine with vegetables used as a side dish, for vegan food, where vegetables and grains play the starring role, think about the style of the dish and its preparation to decide on the appropriate wine. For instance, a spring risotto made with fresh green vegetables favors a delicate white wine, while an earthy grilled portobello mushroom dish demands a bolder red wine. Choose complementary or contrasting flavors, or match the cuisine of a place with a wine from the same region, which will usually be a winning combination. We have paired our entrée recipes here with complementary wines we enjoy. But go ahead—be a wine rebel! Experiment a little. Be adventurous. Throw a wine tasting party. Have everyone bring a bottle—assign a different country, grape, or region to each guest—and serve a variety of finger foods and enjoy!

CANDLE 79'S ORGANIC WINES

Why organic? Conventional vineyards destroy natural land and wildlife and contaminate groundwater and soil with dangerous chemicals. Organic viticulture, practiced without the use of harmful pesticides, nurtures and preserves the soil of the vineyard and helps heal damaged ecosystems. Organic wines are also lower in sulfites.

There's more to good organic wine than just offering protection from harmful chemical additives and high levels of sulfites. At Candle 79 there's a story to be found in every glass. We get to know many of the winemakers, and we're always struck by their passion and the sheer joy they find in sharing their wines. Stellar Winery in South Africa, which makes a luscious dessert Muscat called Heaven on Earth, was the first vineyard in South Africa to be fair-trade certified, and over 25 percent of shares in the winery are owned by the vineyard's workers. At Frog's Leap in Rutherford, California, the winery is 100 percent solar powered, the grapes are dry farmed, their buildings are LEED certified, and their motto is "a healthy soil produces a healthy vine." Dry-farmed grapes encourage the roots of the vines to grow deep into the earth for sustenance. Struggling vines make beautiful wines!

Organic vineyards devise their own creative methods of chemical-free, natural "pest" control. Lolonis Vineyards relies on millions of ladybugs to do the job and have made the ladybug their logo. The trees at Heller Estate are home to majestic owls and colonies of wasps—birds and bugs who do their share of the work at night. We've joked with Henry Heller that it's probably best to avoid the vineyards after dark.

Biodynamic winemakers take it a step further, relating to nature and the vineyard based on good commonsense practices, a consciousness of the uniqueness and climate of each landscape, and a view of the vineyard as a self-sustaining entity. Biodynamic practices include striving to be self-sufficient in energy, using natural fertilizers, working with plants and animals in harmony, and planning the harvest and winemaking based

Heller Estate

on working with nature's rhythms. There is often a healthy dose of spirit and mysticism thrown in for good measure. Think *Farmer's Almanac* meets *The Mists of Avalon* and voila!—you have biodynamic wine. The famed biodynamic winemaker Nicolas Joly often says that "all of life is music!" We'd have to agree, especially when accompanied by a glass of delicious organic wine.

Candle 79's diverse selection of organic, sustainable, and biodynamic wines is the product of environmentally respectful viticulture married with classic artisanal tradition. Our winemakers protect the earth, the people who work in the vineyards, and ultimately our guests from the adverse effects of conventional farming practices. Enjoy a glass of organic wine and experience the true essence of terroir. *À votre santé!*

Francesca MacAaron, Candle 79 manager and vegan wine aficionado

Stuffed Poblano Peppers

Poblano peppers are ideal for stuffing, and they are well-known as the peppers used in the classic Mexican dish chile relleno. They can also be filled with a variety of vegetables, beans, and grains that enhance their rich and velvety taste. Flavorful ancho and mulato chiles are dried versions of poblanos. Served as a main course or a side dish, a platter of poblanos stuffed with a mix of sautéed vegetables and brown rice is picture-perfect for any type of gathering. For a delectable marriage of flavors, serve them with Sautéed Swiss Chard (page 113), as shown here.

6 poblano peppers

3 tablespoons extra-virgin olive oil, plus more for brushing

½ pound oyster mushrooms, chopped

1 bunch scallions, white and green parts, finely chopped

1 cup finely diced zucchini

1 cup fresh corn kernels

½ teaspoon sea salt

1 pound grilled Marinated Tempeh (page 108)

¼ cup chopped red onion

2 cups vegetable stock

1 cup brown rice

½ red bell pepper, seeded and diced

2 cups Roasted Red Bell Pepper and Tomato Sauce (page 119)

Serves 6

Brush the peppers with olive oil. With a long fork or tongs, cook the peppers over an open flame, turning often, until the skin is charred all over, about 5 minutes per side. Put the peppers in a large bowl. Cover with plastic wrap and let cool. Once the peppers are cool, peel off the skins. Make a lengthwise slit in the peppers, discard the seeds, and set aside.

In a sauté pan, heat 2 tablespoons of the olive oil over medium heat. Add the mushrooms and sauté for 5 minutes. Add the scallions, zucchini, corn, and salt and sauté until just tender, 3 to 5 minutes. Add the grilled tempeh and cook for an additional 3 minutes. Mix everything together and let cool.

Meanwhile, put the remaining 1 tablespoon olive oil and the onion, stock, and a pinch of salt in a saucepan. Add the rice and bring to a boil. Decrease the heat, cover, and simmer for 25 minutes. Add the bell pepper and simmer until the rice is just tender, 10 to 15 minutes. Transfer to a large bowl, add the vegetable mixture and mix everything together.

Preheat the oven to 350°F.

Stuff each pepper through the slit with the vegetable and rice mixture. Bake for 15 to 20 minutes, until heated through. Serve at once with the Roasted Red Bell Pepper and Tomato Sauce.

continued

Stuffed Poblano
Peppers, continued

**Holmes Brothers Richmond Plains
Sauvignon Blanc, New Zealand**
Holmes Brothers was the first vineyard in the South Island of
New Zealand to be developed organically. Their Richmond
Plains Sauvignon Blanc is complex and layered with notes of
gooseberry, passion fruit, citrus, and herbs, and lends a bright-
ness to the mushrooms, poblanos, and tempeh.

Spring Vegetable Risotto

Making seasonal risotto is a great way to use fresh vegetables from the farmers' market. Our risotto is rich, creamy, and buttery without the guilt. This risotto also works well as an appetizer or side dish.

4 cups vegetable stock or water
2 tablespoons extra-virgin olive oil
1 clove garlic, chopped
¼ cup finely chopped mushrooms
¼ cup finely chopped zucchini
¼ cup trimmed and sliced fresh
  asparagus
3 tablespoons finely chopped
  shallots
½ teaspoon sea salt
1 cup Arborio rice
½ cup white wine
½ cup chopped fresh flat-leaf
  parsley, for garnish

Serves 4 to 6

Put the stock in a saucepan. Bring to a boil, then decrease the heat to very low heat and hold at a simmer.

Heat 1 tablespoon of the olive oil in a sauté pan over medium heat. Add the garlic, mushrooms, zucchini, and asparagus and sauté until just tender, 3 to 5 minutes. Remove from the heat and set aside.

Heat the remaining tablespoon of olive oil in a large saucepan or soup pot over medium heat. Add the shallots and salt and cook for 1 minute. Add the rice and cook, stirring, until the rice is completely coated, about 2 minutes. Add the wine and cook, stirring, for 5 minutes.

Add ½ cup of the simmering stock to the rice mixture and bring to a boil. Decrease the heat and simmer gently, stirring frequently, until most of the liquid is absorbed. Continue adding the liquid in ½-cup increments and stirring until the rice has absorbed it all, 25 to 30 minutes, stirring in the sautéed vegetables when the rice is about 5 minutes from being done. The rice should be tender but not mushy. Adjust seasoning as needed.

Divide the risotto among large soup bowls, garnish with the parsley, and serve at once.

Loimer Grüner Veltliner, Austria

The Loimer winery, in the Kamptal region, makes wonderfully food-friendly, refreshing but complex "Gru-Vees" that showcase the varietal's typical minerality. Balanced with notes of citrus, melon, grass, and wild herbs, this is a wonderful match for spring vegetables like artichokes and asparagus.

Wild Mushroom and Spring Vegetable Fricassee

We know that spring has arrived in New York when Blooming Hill Farm, an outstanding organic farm in the Hudson Valley, delivers fresh ramps to our kitchen. Ramps are wild onions that have a wonderful, pungent flavor that blends well with other springtime delicacies like fava beans, asparagus, and peas. We add wild mushrooms to the mix to make an incredibly tasty fricassee, and serve it with creamy polenta, as shown in the photo. Brown rice or orzo also make very good accompaniments.

Cashew Parmesan
1 cup cashews
4 tablespoons nutritional yeast
1 tablespoon lemon juice
1 teaspoon salt
Pinch of freshly ground pepper

1 cup fresh fava beans, shelled and rinsed
¼ cup extra-virgin olive oil
1 tablespoon Earth Balance Natural Buttery Spread
1 clove garlic, chopped
1 tablespoon unbleached all-purpose flour
½ cup white wine
2 pounds mixed mushrooms (such as portobello, oyster, chanterelle, and shiitake), stemmed and cut into small pieces
1 pound fresh asparagus, trimmed and cut into 1-inch pieces
1 bunch ramps, trimmed and chopped
½ cup shelled fresh peas
1 teaspoon chopped fresh flat-leaf parsley
1 sprig thyme, chopped
1 teaspoon sea salt
¼ teaspoon freshly ground pepper

Serves 4

To make the Cashew Parmesan, preheat the oven to 250°F. Scatter the cashews on a baking pan and bake for 20 minutes. Put the cashews, nutritional yeast, lemon juice, salt, and pepper in a food processor and process until ground.

Bring a pot of salted water to a boil. Add the fava beans and cook until tender, 3 to 4 minutes. Drain and rinse under cold water. Drain again thoroughly, then peel or pinch off the thin outer skins.

Heat the olive oil and buttery spread in a large sauté pan over medium-high heat. Add the garlic and sauté for 2 minutes. Add the flour and heat until thickened, stirring well, about 2 minutes. Add the wine and stir to incorporate. Add the mushrooms and cook, stirring occasionally, for 5 minutes. Add the reserved fava beans, asparagus, ramps, peas, parsley, thyme, salt, and pepper and cook, stirring and shaking the pan occasionally, until the cooking liquid has evaporated, about 5 minutes.

Serve immediately.

Heller Estate Cachagua Cabernet Sauvignon, California

Heller Estate's dry-farming method produces intensely flavored, concentrated wines that showcase the fruit in the Cabernet varietal. Perfectly balanced with soft tannins and wonderful rich fruit, this elegant Cabernet is a good partner for the wild mushrooms in the fricassee but won't overpower the more delicate vegetables.

Herb-Marinated Grilled Vegetables

A big, beautiful platter of savory grilled vegetables speaks of summer. We serve this dish at the restaurant and for outdoor parties and barbecues as well. For next day's lunch, the leftovers are terrific with grilled bread and a smear of pesto or aioli or a drizzle of good olive oil. Note that the vegetables must marinate for at least 4 hours before grilling.

Herbed Oil Marinade

1½ cups extra-virgin olive oil
1 teaspoon chopped garlic
1 tablespoon nutritional yeast
1 tablespoon chopped fresh chives
2 tablespoons chopped fresh flat-leaf
    parsley
1 tablespoon chopped fresh thyme
    leaves
1 tablespoon chopped fresh oregano
2 tablespoons freshly squeezed
    lemon juice
1 tablespoon grated lemon zest
2 teaspoons sea salt
¼ teaspoon freshly ground pepper

6 whole portobello mushrooms,
    stemmed and sliced
2 zucchini, sliced diagonally
    ¼ inch thick
2 yellow squash, sliced diagonally
    ¼-inch thick
1 large red onion, sliced ½-inch
    thick
3 plum tomatoes, halved

Serves 6 to 8

To make the marinade, whisk the olive oil, garlic, nutritional yeast, chives, parsley, thyme, oregano, lemon juice, lemon zest, salt, and pepper together in a large bowl.

Add the mushrooms, zucchini, squash, onion, and tomatoes to the bowl and toss well to coat. Cover and chill in the refrigerator for at least 4 hours or overnight.

Prepare a very hot gas, charcoal, or stovetop grill and grill the vegetables until grill marks appear, 1 to 2 minutes per side.

Transfer to a platter and serve.

Domaine les Yeuses Syrah, France

This round and juicy Mediterranean Syrah is a "grill's best friend." Its inky fruit and peppery notes with touches of smoky oak give a campfire feel to this rustic grilled vegetable meal.

Moroccan-Spiced Chickpea Cakes

These savory chickpea cakes are packed with flavor thanks to a delicious mélange of spices. They're terrific when served with a drizzle of Red Bell Pepper–Curry Sauce and topped with Apricot Chutney and toasted slivered almonds. We often add kombu, a dried sea vegetable, to the water when cooking dried beans for flavor enhancement and tenderizing. Note that the chickpeas must soak overnight before using.

1 cup dried chickpeas

1-inch piece of kombu

3 to 6 tablespoons extra-virgin olive oil, plus more for brushing

½ cup chopped onion

½ cup chopped celery

⅓ cup unbleached all-purpose flour

2 tablespoons chopped fresh flat-leaf parsley

1 tablespoon smoked paprika

1 tablespoon Old Bay Seasoning

1 teaspoon sea salt

1 teaspoon ground cumin

3 cups Red Bell Pepper–Curry Sauce, for accompaniment (page 117)

1 cup Apricot Chutney, for accompaniment (page 125)

½ cup toasted slivered almonds, for accompaniment

Serves 6

Put the chickpeas in a bowl and add cold water to cover by about 2 inches. Soak for at least 6 hours or overnight in the refrigerator. Drain and rinse.

Place the kombu and chickpeas in a saucepan and add water to cover by 2 inches. Bring to a boil, then decrease the heat, cover, and simmer until tender, about 1 hour. Discard the kombu, then drain, reserving about ½ cup of the cooking liquid.

In a sauté pan, heat 3 tablespoons of the olive oil over medium heat. Add the onion and celery and sauté until softened, about 5 minutes.

Put the chickpeas in a food processor fitted with the metal blade and process until ground. Transfer to a large bowl and add the sautéed vegetables, flour, parsley, paprika, Old Bay Seasoning, salt, and cumin. Add a bit of the reserved cooking liquid from the chickpeas if the mixture seems too dry and crumbly and doesn't stick together. Using your hands, form the mixture into 6 patties about 3 inches in diameter and 1 inch thick.

To bake the patties, preheat the oven to 350°F. Brush a rimmed baking sheet with olive oil and arrange the patties on it. Bake until lightly browned, about 10 minutes per side. If you prefer, pan-fry the patties: Heat 3 tablespoons of olive oil in a sauté pan and fry until golden brown, about 4 minutes per side.

To serve, pour ½ cup of the curry sauce onto each plate. Place a warm cake in the center, top with a dollop of the chutney, and sprinkle with the slivered almonds.

Ampelos Syrache, California

At Ampelos (vine, in Greek) in Santa Barbara County, they are firm believers in the adage that "wine is made in the vineyard." Their "syrache," a spicy blend of Syrah and Grenache, is ripe with notes of cherry, blackberry, and white pepper. The fruit-forward character of this juicy red wine will support the richness of the curry sauce and complement the apricot and spice in the chutney.

Saffron Ravioli with Wild Mushrooms and Cashew Cheese

This pasta dish is fantastic on its own, as well as with tomato sauce, pesto, or cashew cream. It's also terrific topped with crispy fried capers. No matter how you serve it, people are always amazed that the rich, creamy filling uses absolutely no dairy products. Note that you'll need a pasta machine for this recipe, and that the cashews in the filling must soak overnight.

Filling

1 cup raw cashews
2 tablespoons extra-virgin olive oil
¼ cup chopped white onion
¼ teaspoon chopped garlic
¼ cup chopped shallots
¼ cup chopped leek, white and pale
    green parts
½ pound cremini, morel, or
    chanterelle mushrooms,
    stemmed and chopped
1 tablespoon water
1 tablespoons freshly squeezed
    lemon juice
2 tablespoons nutritional yeast
½ teaspoon sea salt

Saffron Pasta

1 teaspoon saffron
2½ cups water
1 cup semolina flour
3 cups unbleached all-purpose flour
3 teaspoons Ener-G egg replacer
¼ teaspoon sea salt
3 tablespoons palm oil, melted
Fine yellow cornmeal or semolina
    flour, for dusting

2½ cups Roasted Plum Tomato
    Sauce (page 116), for serving
Cashew Crème Fraîche (page 125),
    for serving
Minced fresh parsley, for garnish
Crispy Capers (see page 40), for
    garnish

Serves 6 to 8; makes about 30 ravioli

To make the filling, the day before using, put the cashews in a bowl and add enough cold water to cover them. Cover and let soak overnight in the refrigerator.

In a large sauté pan, heat 1 tablespoon of the olive oil over medium heat. Add the onion, garlic, shallots, and leek and sauté until tender, about 5 minutes. Add the mushrooms and cook until their liquid has evaporated, about 10 minutes. Drain well and set aside to cool.

Drain the liquid from the cashews and rinse under cool water. Put the cashews, the remaining 1 tablespoon of olive oil, and the water, lemon juice, nutritional yeast, and salt in a food processor fitted with the metal blade and process until smooth. Add the mushroom mixture and pulse a few times, until the mushrooms are incorporated.

To make the pasta, soak the saffron in the water for about 30 minutes. Put the flours, egg replacer, saffron-infused water, and salt in a stand mixer fitted with the paddle attachment. Add the palm oil and mix well. The dough should be smooth and not stick to your fingers.

Press the dough into a rectangle and roll it, a small section at a time, through a pasta machine. You may have to repeat several times to reach the desired thickness of approximately ⅛ inch. Sprinkle the surface with a small amount of cornmeal or semolina flour to prevent the dough from sticking. Cut the pasta sheets into 2-inch rounds or squares.

continued

To assemble the ravioli, put the pasta pieces on a floured surface. Place a teaspoonful of filling in the center of each square, brush the edges of the dough with a bit of water, top with another piece of pasta, and press the edges with your fingers to seal, and then crimp with a fork. Spray the ravioli with canola oil cooking spray on one side, then flip them over and spray the other side. (If you don't have cooking spray, brush both sides lightly with olive oil.)

Bring a large pot of water to a boil and cook the ravioli until just tender, about 2 minutes.

To serve, spoon the tomato sauce into shallow bowls. Top with alternating layers of ravioli and Cashew Crème Fraîche. Scatter a bit of the parsley over the sauce, top with a spoonful of the capers, and serve at once.

Chiusa Grande Montepulciano d'Abruzzo, Italy

A bright, casual red for hearty at-home suppers, this stainless steel-fermented Montepulciano from Abruzzo tastes of red berries and is scented with violet. Easy drinking with good acidity, this wine is a great regional match for Italian pasta dishes and pizzas.

Variation: Butternut Squash Filling

2½ pounds butternut squash, peeled, seeded, and cut into 2-inch cubes
2 tablespoons extra-virgin olive oil
½ teaspoon ground or freshly grated nutmeg
1 fresh sage leaf, finely chopped
Sea salt

Preheat the oven to 350°F.

Place the butternut squash on a rimmed baking sheet, drizzle with the olive oil, and toss with your hands until evenly coated. Bake the squash for 45 minutes.

Let cool, then transfer to a large bowl. Add the nutmeg and sage and mash until smooth. Season with salt to taste.

Use as an alternative filling for ravioli, following the instructions above.

Manicotti Rustica

Our customers relish this manicotti stuffed with creamy tofu cheese and cremini mushrooms and topped with roasted tomato sauce and pesto. This meat- and dairy-free version is light and lovely and every bit as satisfying as the Italian classic. You can use any type of sheet pasta, including the Saffron Pasta (see page 69) that we use for our ravioli. Both sauces can be made ahead of time.

Tofu Ricotta

1 pound, 5 ounces firm tofu
2 tablespoons nutritional yeast
1 tablespoon extra-virgin olive oil
3 tablespoons freshly squeezed
    lemon juice
1 teaspoon sea salt

4 tablespoons extra-virgin olive oil
1 cup chopped onion
1 pound seitan
2 cups Roasted Plum Tomato Sauce
    (page 116)
½ cup tomato paste
1 tablespoon finely chopped fresh
    basil leaves
1 tablespoon finely chopped fresh
    flat-leaf parsley
1¼ cups water
1 pound cremini mushrooms,
    chopped
Sea salt
12 (6 by 5-inch) sheets of fresh pasta
1½ cups Pesto (page 121), for
    accompaniment
Chopped fresh herbs or
    microgreens, for garnish

Serves 6

To make the Tofu Ricotta, bring a large pot of water to a boil. Decrease the heat, add the tofu, and simmer for 2 minutes. Drain and let cool. Squeeze out as much water as possible from the tofu by pressing between paper towels or using a tofu press.

Put the tofu in a food processor fitted with the metal blade. Add the nutritional yeast, olive oil, lemon juice, and salt and process until smooth, about 3 minutes.

Heat 2 tablespoons of the olive oil in a large sauté pan over medium heat. Add the onions and sauté until softened, about 5 minutes.

Put the seitan in a food processor fitted with the metal blade and process until fairly crumbly, about 2 minutes.

Add the seitan to the sauté pan, along with 1 cup of the tomato sauce and the tomato paste, basil, parsley, and 1 cup of the water. Decrease the heat and simmer, stirring occasionally, until thickened, about 20 minutes. Set aside and let cool.

Heat the remaining 2 tablespoons of olive oil in a large sauté pan over medium heat. Add the mushrooms, season with salt, and cook until softened, about 10 minutes. Set aside.

Preheat the oven to 350°F.

Bring a large a pot of salted water to a boil. Add the pasta sheets and cook until just tender, about 4 minutes. Use a wooden spoon to keep them from sticking to each other. Drain well.

continued

Lay out a pasta sheet with a short side facing you and spread with 2½ tablespoons of the seitan mixture, 2½ tablespoons of the tofu mixture, and 1 tablespoon of the mushrooms. Starting with the short side closer to you, roll into a tube with a slight overlap. Repeat with the remaining ingredients to make 12 stuffed manicotti.

Pour the remaining ¼ cup of water into a large ovenproof baking dish. Arrange the manicotti fold side down in the pan and bake until heated through, about 10 minutes.

Heat the remaining 1 cup of tomato sauce.

Divide the manicotti among 6 plates. Top each serving with generous spoonfuls of the pesto and tomato sauce. Garnish with the chopped fresh herbs and serve at once.

Salustri Marleo Sangiovese, Italy

The Salustri family has been part of the farming landscape of the Tuscan hills of Poggi del Sasso since the 1200s. Say the Salustris, "We only know the organic way because our father never knew any other way." This big and bold Sangiovese complements rich seitan-based ragouts.

Potato Gnocchi

Bart Potenza, Candle's founder, grew up in an Italian-American home, and he is no stranger to delicious, authentic Italian cooking. He's wild about this gnocchi dish, which can be served as an appetizer or entrée. These little gems are so easy to prepare—just make sure that the potatoes are very tender. Our gnocchi freeze well and keep in the freezer for up to 2 months, but they will disappear quicker than that.

3 large Idaho potatoes
1 teaspoon sea salt
1 tablespoon extra-virgin olive oil
1½ cups unbleached all-purpose flour, plus more for dusting
1½ cups Pesto (page 121) or Roasted Plum Tomato Sauce (page 116), for serving
½ cup thinly sliced fresh basil leaves, for garnish

Serves 8 as an appetizer, or 4 as an entrée

Preheat the oven to 350°F.

Wrap the potatoes in aluminum foil, place on a baking sheet, and bake until very tender, about 1 hour and 30 minutes. Remove from the oven and let cool a bit (potatoes should still be warm to work with).

Halve the potatoes and scoop the flesh into a bowl. Discard the peels. Grate the pieces of flesh so the gnocchi won't be lumpy. Mash with a spoon or potato masher for a few seconds.

continued

Add the salt, oil, and flour and mix with your hands for about 2 minutes, or until the mixture forms a smooth ball.

Divide the mixture into 4 balls. On a floured surface, roll each ball out into a long rope about ¾ inch thick. Cut into ½-inch pieces. The uncooked gnocchi can be frozen at this point: Put the pieces on a tray or baking sheet so they don't stick together, cover with plastic wrap, and freeze. Once frozen, place them in a plastic container or heavy-duty ziplock freezer bag and store in the freezer for up to 2 months. Use as needed, cooking as directed, below.

Bring about 8 cups of water to a boil, then gently drop the gnocchi into the pot. They will rise to the top when they are done, about 3 minutes (or 5 minutes if frozen). Remove with a strainer or slotted spoon. Spoon the gnocchi into shallow pasta or soup bowls, top with the desired sauce, garnish with the basil, and serve.

Chamisal Stainless Steel Chardonnay, California

Chamisal was the very first vineyard planted in the Edna Valley. Chamisal has crafted this special wine, untouched by oak, to express the pure essence of Chardonnay. Tropical fruit flavors combine with notes of ripe lemon and grapefruit to create a full but refreshing wine that complements the earthy and buttery notes in these delicate little pillows. The Chardonnay will complement the gnocchi when served with a lighter sauce, such as a pesto or cashew cream. If you serve them with a heartier, tomato-based sauce or ragout, try an Italian red, like Chianti.

Pan-Seared Pine Nut Pesto Tofu

In the restaurant, we serve this rich and tasty tofu dish with Roasted Fingerling Potatoes (page 102) and Sautéed Royal Trumpet Mushrooms (page 110). We also make delicious summer sandwiches with this tofu, roasted red bell peppers, and pesto on slices of grilled country bread. Note that the tofu must marinate for at least 4 hours before using.

Pesto Marinade

1 cup pine nuts
3 tablespoons extra-virgin olive oil
2 tablespoons freshly squeezed
   lemon juice
1 cup water
2 cups chopped fresh flat-leaf parsley
3 cups fresh basil leaves
2 cloves garlic
3 tablespoons nutritional yeast
½ teaspoon sea salt

2 pounds extra-firm tofu, sliced into
   1 by 2 by 3-inch pieces
2 tablespoons extra-virgin olive oil

Serves 4 to 6

To make the marinade, put the pine nuts, olive oil, lemon juice, and water in a blender and process to form a chunky puree. Add the parsley, basil, garlic, nutritional yeast, and salt, and process for 1 minute.

In a large pot, bring about 3 quarts of water to a boil. Add the tofu, decrease the heat, and simmer for 2 minutes. Drain the tofu well, then transfer to a large, nonreactive, ovenproof baking dish. Pour the marinade over it, cover, and let marinate in the refrigerator for at least 4 hours or overnight. Turn the tofu occasionally.

Remove the tofu from the marinade and reserve the marinade. Heat the olive oil in a large sauté pan over low heat. Add the tofu and cook until lightly browned, about 2 minutes per side.

To serve, heat the marinade and spoon a bit of it in the center of a plate, then top with the warm tofu.

Lolonis Fumé Blanc, California

Lolonis Vineyards in the Redwood Valley is known by many for "that delicious ladybug wine." As part of their pioneering organic pest control program, over five million ladybugs are released in the vineyards every summer. The full body and fruit in their Fumé Blanc complement the buttery fingerling potatoes of the side dish, while the notes of lemongrass and zesty acidity add a contrasting freshness that picks up the summery notes of the basil.

Chile-Grilled Tofu with Avocado-Tomatillo Sauce

The chile sauce in this recipe is a fantastic marinade for tofu, tempeh, or seitan. At Candle 79, we serve this dish with a side of Quinoa-Vegetable Pilaf (page 107). The deep, smoky flavors with a hint of spiciness evince the classic Southwestern style. The tofu is also great served with Watercress, Jicama, and Corn Salad with Jalapeño Dressing (page 43), as illustrated here. Note that the tofu must marinate for at least 4 hours before using.

Chile Sauce

5 guajillo chiles
⅓ cup plus 2 tablespoons extra-virgin olive oil
½ cup chopped onion
¼ teaspoon chipotle chile powder
¼ teaspoon ground cumin
½ teaspoon smoked paprika
½ cup chopped fresh cilantro
1 tablespoon tomato paste
2 tablespoons freshly squeezed lemon juice
1 teaspoon sea salt
1 cup water

2 pounds extra-firm tofu, sliced into 1 by 1 by 2-inch pieces

Avocado-Tomatillo Sauce

2 cups tomatillos, husked and rinsed
1 tablespoon extra-virgin olive oil
1 clove garlic, chopped
1 jalapeño pepper, seeded and diced
½ cup chopped fresh cilantro
1 ripe avocado, halved, pitted, peeled, and chopped
1 cup water
1 tablespoon sea salt

Sprouts or microgreens, for garnish

Serves 6

To make the Chile Sauce, put the guajillo chiles in a bowl and cover with hot water. Soak for 15 minutes to reconstitute. Drain and chop.

Heat the 2 tablespoons of olive oil in a sauté pan over medium heat. Add the onion and sauté until softened, 3 to 5 minutes. Let cool, then transfer to a blender. Add the chopped chiles, chipotle powder, cumin, paprika, cilantro, tomato paste, lemon juice, salt, water, and the ⅓ cup of olive oil and process until very smooth.

In a large pot, bring about 3 quarts of water to a boil. Add the tofu, decrease the heat, and simmer for 2 minutes. Drain the tofu well, then transfer to a large, nonreactive, ovenproof baking dish. Pour the Chile Sauce over it, cover, and let marinate in the refrigerator for at least 4 hours or overnight. Turn the tofu occasionally.

To make the Avocado-Tomatillo Sauce, preheat the oven to 350°F. Put the tomatillos on a rimmed baking sheet, drizzle with the olive oil, and roast for 15 minutes. Let cool, then transfer to a blender. Add the garlic, jalapeño pepper, cilantro, avocado, water, and salt and process until smooth.

Prepare a medium-hot gas or charcoal grill. Remove the tofu from the sauce, reserving the sauce for garnish. Grill the tofu until grill marks appear, about 2 minutes per side.

To serve, spoon a bit of the Avocado-Tomatillo Sauce in the center of a plate and top with the grilled tofu. Garnish with the reserved sauce and the sprouts and serve warm.

Rapp Weingut "Sunshine" Sylvaner Blend, Germany

The small, picturesque Rapp winery, surrounded by fields of sunflowers, is located in the heart of the Nahe River region. This luscious blend of Sylvaner and Müller-Thurgau tastes like liquid sunshine, candied citrus, and white flowers, with a refreshingly dry finish. It both cools the spice of the grilled tofu and accentuates the savory qualities in the avocado sauce.

Live Lasagna

Some people believe that fruits, vegetables, nuts, seeds, and grains are better to eat raw, or "live," because cooking diminishes the amount of vitamins, minerals, and enzymes. This "live" take on lasagna is made with raw vegetables and nut cheese. Note that the nuts must soak overnight.

Cashew Cheese

3 cups raw cashews
2 tablespoons nutritional yeast
1 tablespoon freshly squeezed lemon
    juice
1 tablespoon extra-virgin olive oil
2 tablespoons water
6 basil leaves, finely sliced
1 tablespoon parsley

Tomato Sauce

2 large ripe tomatoes, coarsely
    chopped
½ teaspoon chopped shallot
1 tablespoon extra-virgin olive oil
1 fresh basil leaf
Sea salt and freshly ground pepper

¼ pound oyster mushrooms
1 shallot, thinly sliced
3 scallions, white and green parts,
    thinly sliced
2 tablespoons freshly squeezed
    lemon juice
2 to 3 tablespoons extra-virgin olive
    oil, plus more for drizzling
Sea salt and freshly ground pepper
1 large zucchini, trimmed and
    halved crosswise
2½ pounds heirloom tomatoes,
    sliced crosswise
1½ cups Pesto (page 121)
Microgreens, for garnish
Edible flowers, for garnish

Serves 4 to 6

To make the Cashew Cheese, the day before serving, put the cashews in a bowl and add enough cold water to cover them. Cover and let soak overnight in the refrigerator.

Rinse and drain the nuts and transfer to a food processor fitted with the metal blade. Add the nutritional yeast, lemon juice, olive oil, and water and process until smooth. With a spatula, scrape the edges of the food processor to ensure that everything is fully puréed. Fold in the basil and parsley.

To make the sauce, put the tomatoes, shallot, olive oil, and basil in a blender. Pulse 2 or 3 times to make a chunky sauce. Season with salt and pepper to taste.

In a small bowl, combine the mushrooms, shallot, scallions, lemon juice, and 2 tablespoons of the olive oil. Stir well and season with salt and pepper to taste.

Using a mandoline or a very sharp knife, slice the zucchini halves lengthwise into very thin strips.

To assemble each serving of lasagna, pour some of the tomato sauce in the center of a plate. Lay 3 slices of zucchini over the sauce and top with a spoonful each of the nut cheese and the mushroom mixture. Add another layer of zucchini, nut cheese, and mushrooms. Top with the tomato slices, garnish with the pesto, and drizzle with olive oil. Garnish with the microgreens and edible flowers and serve at once.

Do Ferreiro Albariño, Spain

From the western part of Spain near the Atlantic, Do Ferreiro Albariño is sunny, vibrant, bracing, and fresh. Tart orchard fruits, lemon zest, and wild, green herbal notes work beautifully with the summery, garden-fresh flavors in this raw lasagna.

Tempeh Cakes

These robust cakes, which can be prepared up to 3 days in advance, are a great item to serve for a dinner party. The nutty and smoky flavors develop and combine beautifully, and taste wonderful with vibrant Blood Orange–Fennel Salad (page 52) and our Zucchini Blossom Sauce (page 122). Note that the cannellini beans must soak overnight before using.

1 cup dried cannellini beans
7 cups water
1-inch piece of kombu
2 bay leaves
1 cup brown rice
1 tablespoon extra-virgin olive oil
2 bay leaves
Pinch of sea salt
6 tablespoons extra-virgin olive oil
½ cup diced shallots
2 tablespoons tomato paste
1 teaspoon smoked paprika
2 tablespoons chopped fresh flat-leaf
    parsley
¼ teaspoon sea salt
1 pound baked Marinated Tempeh,
    cubed (page 108)

Serves 6

To make the beans, the day before using, put the beans in a bowl, and add cold water to cover by 2 inches. Cover and soak overnight in the refrigerator. Drain and rinse.

Bring 4 cups of the water to a boil in a saucepan, then add the beans, kombu and bay leaves. Decrease the heat, cover, and simmer until tender, 30 to 40 minutes. Drain the beans, reserving 1 cup of the cooking liquid. Discard the bay leaves and kombu and set the beans aside to cool.

Meanwhile, make the rice. Put the rice, the remaining 3 cups of water, olive oil, bay leaves, and salt in another saucepan. Bring to a boil, then decrease the heat, stir once, cover, and simmer until the liquid is absorbed and rice is tender, 20 to 30 minutes. Remove the bay leaves and set the rice aside to cool.

Heat 3 tablespoons of the olive oil in a large sauté pan over medium heat. Add the shallots and sauté for 3 to 5 minutes. Add the tomato paste and cook, stirring, until evenly combined. Add the paprika, parsley, and salt and cook, stirring, for 2 minutes.

Add the tempeh, beans, rice, and ½ cup of the reserved bean cooking liquid and cook, stirring occasionally, for 5 to 8 minutes, adding more cooking liquid if the mixture seems too thick and not moist enough to stick together. Set aside to cool slightly.

When the tempeh mixture is cool enough to handle, use your hands to form and press the mixture into 6 cakes about 3 inches in diameter and 1 inch thick.

Heat the remaining 3 tablespoons of olive oil in a sauté pan and cook the cakes over medium heat until golden brown, about 3 minutes per side. Serve warm.

Domaine des Cèdres Côtes du Rhône, France

Domaine des Cèdres is located in a small commune in the Southern Rhône Valley, home to the famous mistral winds. This classic blend of Grenache, Syrah, Carignan, and Cinsault tastes of earth, summer berries, cedar, and spice and is a great complement to the nutty richness and fresh herbs of the tempeh cake.

Tempeh with Mole Sauce

The word mole *is derived from the ancient Mexican word* molli, *meaning "concoction." While many mole sauces are based on homemade broth made from meat or poultry, this version, with its deep, rich flavors, is made with onion, plantain, nuts, seeds, dried chiles, herbs and spices, vegetable stock, and dark chocolate. Look for pasilla, mulato, and ancho chiles in Latin American markets. Sweet Potato Mash (page 101) and Braised Green Beans (page 111) are excellent accompaniments to this dish, as illustrated here.*

5 tablespoons extra-virgin olive oil
1 cup chopped onion
1 clove garlic, chopped
½ cup raisins
¼ cup blanched slivered almonds
2 tablespoons white sesame seeds
½ plantain, sliced
1 pasilla chile, seeded and chopped
1 mulato chile, seeded and chopped
1 ancho chile, seeded and chopped
Sprig of thyme
⅛ teaspoon chopped fresh oregano
Pinch of ground cinnamon
½ teaspoon ground cloves
1 teaspoon sea salt
3 cups vegetable stock
⅓ cup vegan dark chocolate chips
   or pieces
1 pound baked Marinated Tempeh,
   cut into 2 by 2-inch pieces
   (page 108)
Microgreens, for garnish
2 shallots, thinly sliced, for garnish

Serves 4 to 6

Preheat the oven to 350°F.

Heat 3 tablespoons of the olive oil in a large sauté pan over medium heat. Add the onion, garlic, raisins, almonds, sesame seeds, and plantain, decrease the heat to medium-low, and sauté for 5 minutes. Add the chiles, thyme, oregano, cinnamon, cloves, and salt and stir well to combine. Stir in the stock and simmer, stirring often, for about 20 minutes.

Add the chocolate and stir until melted. Remove the sauce from the heat and let cool for about 30 minutes. It should still be a little warm. Transfer to a blender and process until smooth.

Put the tempeh pieces in an ovenproof baking dish, pour the sauce over them, and stir to coat. Let the mixture sit for 15 to 20 minutes. Cover with aluminum foil and bake for 10 minutes.

Heat the remaining 2 tablespoons of olive oil in a sauté pan over medium-high heat. Add the shallots and sauté for 2 minutes.

Garnish the tempeh pieces with the microgreens and shallots. Serve at once.

Lolonis Zinfandel, California

Lolonis wines, crafted in the Redwood Valley, are true artisanal expressions of terroir, and their Zinfandel is a best seller at Candle 79's bar. Deep blackberry fruit, warm spice, and toasted cocoa notes make this jammy Zin a match made in heaven for smoky, chocolaty mole sauce and savory sweet potatoes.

Nori- and Sesame-Crusted Seitan

The seitan in this Asian-influenced dish is marinated in toasted sesame oil and a mélange of fresh herbs and dredged in a flour-nori-sesame mixture to make beautifully crusted cutlets. We usually serve this ever-popular dish with Gingered Sugar Snap Peas (page 112), Soba Noodles (page 105) or Jasmine Rice (page 106), and Edamame-Mint Sauce (page 124), as pictured here. We also garnish the dish with julienned watermelon radishes and scallion to add a layer of flavor and crunch. It's a fabulous combination of tastes. Note that the cutlets must marinate for at least 3 hours.

Marinade

2 tablespoons plus ¾ teaspoon
    grapeseed oil
½ white onion, chopped
1½ teaspoons toasted sesame oil
1 cup chopped fresh cilantro
½ cup chopped fresh mint leaves
½ teaspoon red pepper flakes
2 cups water
1 tablespoon white miso
1 teaspoon sea salt

6 to 8 seitan cutlets (about
    1½ pounds; page 109)

Crust

1 cup unbleached all-purpose flour
2 nori sheets, broken up into small
    pieces
½ cup white sesame seeds
½ teaspoon red pepper flakes
½ teaspoon sea salt

4 to 6 tablespoons grapeseed or
    safflower oil, for frying

Serves 6

To make the marinade, heat the grapeseed oil in a sauté pan over medium heat. Add the onion and sauté until softened, about 3 minutes. Remove from the heat and let cool. Put the onion, sesame oil, cilantro, mint, red pepper flakes, water, miso, and salt in a blender and process until smooth.

Put the cutlets in a nonreactive bowl or pan. Pour the marinade over the cutlets, coating them well. Cover and let marinate in the refrigerator for at least 3 hours or overnight.

To make the crust, put the flour, nori, sesame seeds, red pepper flakes, and salt in a large bowl, making sure that the nori is crushed into the mixture.

Drain the seitan, squeeze out the excess liquid, and discard the marinade. Dredge the cutlets in the crust mixture, pressing it into the seitan with your hands to ensure that the seitan is completely covered.

In a large sauté pan, heat 4 tablespoons of the oil over medium heat until the oil is hot but not smoking. Add the cutlets and cook until golden brown, about 1 to 2 minutes per side. Add more oil as needed to cook all of the cutlets. Drain on paper towels and serve at once.

Biokult Sparkling Rosé, Austria

This sparkling Pinot Noir comes from a co-op of organic growers in Austria. Slightly sweet sparkling wines can be the perfect accompaniment to Asian-influenced dishes. The subtle notes of peach and cassis in this lively sparkler pair beautifully with the garden-fresh mint and cilantro in the marinade.

Panko-Crusted Seitan Milanese

We serve seitan cutlets in the same Milanese-style that meat dishes are often served. The seitan is marinated in a fragrant garlic, olive oil, and lemon-basil bath, then the cutlets are breaded with panko and lightly pan-fried. Garden-fresh arugula and heirloom tomatoes top off this beautiful entrée.

Marinade
6 tablespoons extra-virgin olive oil
½ white onion, chopped
2 cloves garlic, thinly sliced
½ cup water
2 tablespoons freshly squeezed
    lemon juice
1 cup fresh basil leaves
¼ cup coarsely chopped fresh flat-
    leaf parsley
1 teaspoon Ener-G egg replacer
1 teaspoon sea salt
¼ teaspoon freshly ground pepper

6 to 8 seitan cutlets (about
    1½ pounds; page 109)
1 cup panko bread crumbs
1 teaspoon Ener-G egg replacer
2 tablespoons extra-virgin olive oil

Topping
1 small bunch arugula, stemmed
    and chopped
2 heirloom tomatoes, coarsely
    chopped
1 tablespoon extra-virgin olive oil
1 teaspoon balsamic vinegar

Serves 6

To make the marinade, heat 2 tablespoons of the olive oil in a sauté pan over medium heat. Add the onion and garlic and sauté until softened, 3 to 5 minutes. Let cool, then transfer to a blender. Add the remaining 4 tablespoons of olive oil and the water, lemon juice, basil, parsley, egg replacer, salt, and pepper and process until smooth.

Put the seitan in a nonreactive baking dish, pour the marinade over it, cover, and marinate in the refrigerator for at least 4 hours or overnight.

To prepare the cutlets, fill a rimmed plate, shallow bowl, or plastic bag with the panko and egg replacer and stir to combine. Remove the cutlets from the marinade. Dredge the cutlets in the panko mixture, shaking off any excess and pressing the panko mixture firmly into the seitan.

To pan-fry the cutlets, heat the 2 tablespoons of olive oil in a large sauté pan over medium heat until hot but not smoking. Add the cutlets and fry until crisp, about 3 minutes per side, adding more oil if necessary. Drain on paper towels. Alternatively, to bake the cutlets, preheat the oven to 350°F. Spray a baking sheet with olive oil spray, put the cutlets on the pan, and bake for 15 to 20 minutes, until golden brown.

To make the topping, in a large bowl toss the arugula, tomatoes, olive oil, and vinegar together to coat.

To serve, spoon a heaping portion of the arugula-tomato mixture on top of each cutlet and serve at once.

Kawarau Sauvignon Blanc, New Zealand
Located beneath the magnificent Pisa Range in the heart of Central Otago, Kawarau produces adventurous, distinctive organic wines full of true Kiwi character. Their Sauvignon Blanc displays citrus, sunshine, and flinty minerality and is the perfect match for the acidity of tomatoes and balsamic vinegar.

Sofrito-Seared Seitan

Joy loves this dish. The fragrance of tomatoes roasting in the oven for Sofrito Sauce conjures up aromatic kitchen memories from the past for her. We marinate and cook seitan in this savory sauce and serve it with rice and avocados. Note that the seitan cutlets must marinate for at least 2 hours.

Sofrito Sauce
4 plum tomatoes, halved
½ cup chopped white onion
½ cup chopped red onion
1 clove garlic, chopped
2 red bell peppers, seeded and
    chopped
3 tablespoons chopped fresh cilantro
1 tablespoon chopped fresh flat-leaf
    parsley
½ teaspoon chopped fresh oregano
4 tablespoons extra-virgin olive oil,
    plus more for brushing
2 tablespoons freshly squeezed
    lemon juice
1 tablespoon white wine vinegar
2 teaspoons sea salt
¾ teaspoon freshly ground pepper

6 to 8 seitan cutlets (about
    1½ pounds; page 109)
2 tablespoons extra-virgin olive oil

Serves 6

To make the sauce, preheat the oven to 350°F. Brush a rimmed baking sheet with olive oil and arrange the tomatoes, cut side up, on it. Roast until softened, about 20 minutes. Let cool, then peel the tomatoes, reserving any juices.

Put the tomatoes and their juices and the onions, garlic, peppers, cilantro, parsley, oregano, olive oil, lemon juice, vinegar, salt, and pepper in a food processor fitted with the metal blade and process to form a chunky sauce.

Put the seitan cutlets in a shallow nonreactive bowl or pan. Pour the sauce over the cutlets, making sure they are well coated. Cover and let marinate in the refrigerator for 2 to 4 hours. Remove the cutlets and reserve the sauce.

In a large nonstick sauté pan, heat the olive oil over medium heat. Add the cutlets and cook until lightly browned, about 2 minutes per side. Add the sauce to the pan and let simmer until heated through, about 5 minutes. Serve at once.

Manifesto! Sauvignon Blanc, California

Manifesto "Earth First" sustainable wines are made in California with a message, clearly stated on their website: "Get our hands in the vineyard dirt and know our growers. Make wine that doesn't cost a fortune. Make wine that complements, not overpowers." Their Sauvignon Blanc is delightfully versatile, with a bracing dose of food-friendly acidity, and flavors of juicy orange creamsicle and kiwifruit. A natural choice with fried plantains, and a fine match for smoky soffrito.

Seitan Piccata

Candle 79's rendition of classic Seitan Piccata takes veganism to a whole new level. This easy, elegant entrée is made with a delicate sauce of white wine, shallots, and fresh parsley, among other good things. Caper berries are oblong, green fruits from the caper plant. More mild than caper buds, they still pack a lemony punch, especially because they are pickled. We like to serve this dish with Potato Cakes (page 103) and Creamed Spinach (page 114), as shown here.

6 seitan cutlets (about 1½ pounds; page 109)
Whole wheat flour, for dredging
6 tablespoons extra-virgin olive oil
¼ cup minced shallots
¼ cup finely sliced leek, white and pale green parts
1 teaspoon sea salt
½ teaspoon freshly ground pepper
1 tablespoon unbleached all-purpose flour
¾ cup white wine
¼ cup capers, drained
2 cups vegetable stock or water
1 bay leaf
1 tablespoon minced fresh flat-leaf parsley, plus ¼ cup chopped fresh flat-leaf parsley for garnish (optional)
1 teaspoon minced fresh thyme leaves
⅛ teaspoon ground turmeric
¼ cup freshly squeezed lemon juice
Caper berries, for garnish
1 lemon, thinly sliced, for garnish (optional)

Serves 6

Dredge the cutlets in the whole wheat flour, shaking off any excess.

Heat 2 tablespoons of the olive oil in a large sauté pan over high heat. Add the cutlets and cook until crisp and golden brown, 1 to 2 minutes per side. Place the cutlets on individual plates or a platter.

Heat the remaining 4 tablespoons of olive oil in another sauté pan over medium heat. Add the shallots, leek, salt, and pepper and sauté until soft and translucent, 5 to 7 minutes. Add the all-purpose flour and cook for 2 minutes, stirring constantly, to make a roux. Add the wine to deglaze the pan and stir well to incorporate the flour. Add the capers, stock, bay leaf, minced parsley, thyme, turmeric, and lemon juice and cook over medium heat until the sauce becomes slightly glossy, about 10 minutes.

Spoon the sauce onto serving plates and place the cutlets atop the sauce. Garnish with the caper berries and the optional chopped parsley and lemon slices. Serve at once.

Bonterra Chardonnay, California

In picturesque Mendocino County, Bonterra has been proudly certified organic since 1987. The full body and toasty oak in this Chardonnay echo the silky texture of the lemon-caper sauce.

Tamarind-Barbecued Seitan

Tamarind is a pod from the tamarind tree, which grows in tropical climates, and tamarind paste is a common ingredient used in Thai, Indian, Caribbean, and Mediterranean cooking. It is available at Asian and Indian markets and online. Our sweet-and-sour barbecue sauce made with tart tamarind paste is out of this world. It's great for cooking and can also be used in the Barbecued Black-Eyed Peas (page 100)—which is why these two are great to make together! We also serve this dish with Sautéed Swiss Chard (page 113)and Sweet Potato Mash (page 101). For summertime barbecue feasts we add fresh corn on the cob, cornbread, and coleslaw. Note that the seitan cutlets must marinate for at least 2 hours.

Tamarind Barbecue Sauce
½ cup water
½ cup ketchup
⅓ cup grapeseed oil
⅓ cup molasses
⅓ cup maple syrup
¼ cup tamari
4 tablespoons tamarind paste
2 tablespoons tomato paste
2 tablespoons brown rice vinegar
2 tablespoons apple cider vinegar
1 tablespoon chopped fresh ginger
1 teaspoon coriander seeds
Pinch of sea salt
Pinch of chipotle chile powder

6 to 8 seitan cutlets (about
    1½ pounds; page 109)
3 tablespoons extra-virgin olive oil

Serves 6

To make the sauce, put the water, ketchup, grapeseed oil, molasses, maple syrup, tamari, tamarind paste, tomato paste, vinegars, ginger, coriander, salt, and chipotle powder in a blender and process until very smooth. Pour the mixture into a saucepan and simmer over very low heat for 10 minutes.

Put the seitan in a nonreactive baking dish. Pour the barbecue sauce over it, cover, and let marinate in the refrigerator for at least 2 hours or overnight.

To cook the seitan, heat the olive oil in a large sauté pan over medium heat. Remove the cutlets from the sauce, letting the excess drip off and reserving the sauce for another use (see headnote). Add the seitan to the pan and cook until golden brown, 2 to 3 minutes per side, adding more oil if needed. The seitan can also be grilled over medium heat until golden brown, 2 to 3 minutes per side.

Serve immediately.

Frog's Leap Cabernet Sauvignon, California

Frog's Leap is a progressive, sustainable Eden in Rutherford, headquartered in a big, historic red barn. As they state on their website, the people of Frog's Leap believe that "a healthy soil produces a healthy vine," and they run their vineyards according to their mantras of "reduce, reuse, recycle, retain, and revere." Juicy plum, dried herbs, cedar, and vanilla notes in this Bordeaux-style cabernet make the spicy-tangy tamarind flavors of the barbecue sauce sing.

Paella

This vegan version of the Spanish classic paella is made with saffron-scented vegetables and seitan sausage—we love artisan grain-based sausage from Field Roast Grain Meat Co. (see Resources, page 182). When making this dish, cook the rice until it crackles and becomes toasty to make a socarrat, the crispy layer that marks a true paella. Served with a Spanish Tempranillo, Rioja, or cava, this is a wonderful dish to make for a hungry crowd.

2 ears of fresh corn, husked
1¼ teaspoons saffron
1 cup hot water
3 tablespoons extra-virgin olive oil
½ pound oyster mushrooms, stemmed and chopped
2½ teaspoons sea salt, plus more for sautéing
Freshly ground pepper
½ cup chopped white onion
2 cloves garlic, thinly sliced
1 red bell pepper, seeded and chopped
1 green bell pepper, seeded and chopped
1¼ teaspoons smoked paprika
1 cup chopped cauliflower florets
1 cup chopped tomatoes
3 to 4 cups vegetable stock
2 cups Valencia or Arborio rice
1 cup ground seitan sausage, cut diagonally into 1-inch pieces
½ cup chopped scallions, white and green parts (optional)
Lemon wedges, for garnish

Serves 6

Using tongs, hold the corn over a gas flame and cook, turning, until nicely charred. When cool enough to handle, cut the kernels off the cobs and set aside.

Soak the saffron in the hot water for at least 15 minutes.

Heat 1 tablespoon of the olive oil in a large sauté pan over medium heat. Add the mushrooms, season with salt and pepper, and sauté for 5 minutes. Transfer to a large bowl and set aside.

Using the same pan, heat another 1 tablespoon of the olive oil over medium heat. Add the onion, garlic, bell peppers, and 1 teaspoon of the smoked paprika and sauté until just tender, about 3 minutes. Add the corn, cauliflower, and tomatoes and cook, stirring occasionally, for about 5 minutes. Remove from the heat and add to the mushrooms.

Heat the stock in a saucepan and hold it at a simmer. Heat the remaining tablespoon of olive oil in a soup pot or traditional paella pan over medium heat. Add the rice and stir until well coated, about 30 seconds. Add the salt and the saffron water and cook, stirring, until it is absorbed. Add ½ cup of the simmering stock to the rice and cook, stirring, until the rice has absorbed it all. Continue adding the liquid in ½-cup increments and stirring until the rice has absorbed it, until the rice is tender, not mushy, and retains its bite, 25 to 30 minutes.

continued

To get the *socarrat*, or caramelized crust on the rice, uncover the pot and increase the heat to high. Cook until the rice crackles and smells toasty, being careful not to burn it. Add the mushroom mixture and sausage and stir. Cook over medium heat, scraping the bottom of the pot so the rice doesn't stick, for about 3 minutes.

Remove from the heat, cover with a kitchen towel, and let rest for 10 minutes. Taste and adjust the seasonings if necessary.

Sprinkle the paella with the remaining ¼ teaspoon of smoked paprika and the optional scallions. Garnish with the lemon wedges and serve.

Viña Sastre Roble Tempranillo, Spain

Hermanos Sastre is a family-run winery in the heart of the Ribera del Duero, Spain's most revered wine region. Ripe red currants, sweet oak, and a touch of spice make this Tempranillo an authentic pairing for the rich but piquant flavors of vegan paella.

Spaghetti and Seitan Wheatballs with Roasted Plum Tomato Sauce

Our vegan version of this American classic is one of our most popular main courses and one of the easiest to make. This spaghetti and "wheatball" dish is ideal for a family supper or a cozy dinner party. Although we invented this dish for kids, it's always eaten up by the grown-ups.

Seitan Wheatballs

1 tablespoon extra-virgin olive oil, plus more for brushing
4 cloves garlic or black garlic, chopped
1 shallot, chopped
½ cup diced onion
½ cup diced celery
1 pound seitan
¼ teaspoon red pepper flakes
1 teaspoon chopped fresh flat-leaf parsley
½ teaspoon sea salt
⅓ cup unbleached all-purpose flour

1 pound spaghetti
1½ cups Roasted Plum Tomato Sauce (page 116)
Fresh basil leaves, for garnish

Serves 4 to 6

Preheat the oven to 350°F. Brush a rimmed baking sheet with olive oil.

To make the wheatballs, heat the olive oil in a sauté pan over medium heat. Add the garlic, shallots, onion, and celery and sauté until softened, about 5 minutes. Set aside to cool.

Put the seitan in a food processor fitted with the metal blade and process until completely ground. Add the red pepper flakes, parsley, and salt and pulse to incorporate. Add the sautéed onion and celery and process until completely ground.

Transfer the seitan mixture to a large bowl and stir in the flour. Roll the mixture into 1-inch balls and put them on the prepared baking sheet. There should be about 16 balls. Brush the balls with olive oil and put 2 tablespoons of water into the baking pan.

Cover with aluminum foil and bake for 25 to 30 minutes. Remove from the oven.

Meanwhile, bring a large pot of water to a boil and cook the spaghetti until just tender, 8 to 10 minutes. Drain well. Heat the tomato sauce on the stovetop until warm and bubbly.

Portion the pasta into individual bowls and top each serving with tomato sauce and wheatballs. Garnish with the basil and serve warm.

Nuova Cappelletta Barbera Minola, Italy

Barbera is one of the classic varietals of Italy's Piedmont, often found on the tables of village trattorias serving simple, rustic local cuisine. Ripe red fruit, bright acidity, and low tannins make this beautifully balanced, biodynamic Barbera a perfect choice for tomato-based sauces.

Black Bean–Chipotle Burgers

Burgers and fries are a perennial lunchtime favorite. At Candle 79, we spice our hearty bean- and rice-based burger with the rich and smoky flavors of chipotle chile powder and smoked paprika. We top it with slices of creamy avocado and serve it with a side of Polenta Fries (page 104) and no one ever misses the meat. Note that the dried beans must soak for at least 6 hours.

1½ cups dried black beans, rinsed and picked over
1-inch piece of kombu
2 cups chopped yellow onions
1 teaspoon chipotle chile powder
3 bay leaves
2 teaspoons salt
Pinch of freshly ground pepper
1½ cups brown rice
3 cups water
1 tablespoon extra-virgin olive oil, plus more as needed
1 cup raw pumpkin seeds
1 tablespoon smoked paprika
6 to 8 burger rolls
1 red onion, thinly sliced (optional)
Avocado slices, for serving (optional)

Makes 6 to 8 burgers

Put the beans in a saucepan or bowl and add cold water to cover by about 2 inches. Cover and soak for at least 6 hours or overnight in the refrigerator. Drain and rinse.

Put the beans, kombu, onions, chipotle powder, bay leaves, 1 teaspoon of the salt, and the pepper in a large saucepan. Add water to cover by 3 inches and bring to a boil. Decrease the heat, cover, and simmer until the beans are tender, about 1½ to 2 hours. Most of the liquid should be absorbed by the beans, but add a bit more water if they seem too dry. Drain the beans, reserving the cooking liquid. Discard the kombu and bay leaves.

Meanwhile, put the rice and a pinch of salt in a saucepan and add the water. Bring to a boil, then decrease the heat, stir once, cover, and simmer until all of the water is absorbed and the rice is tender, 35 to 40 minutes. Remove from the heat and let stand, covered, for 10 minutes.

Heat the olive oil in a sauté pan over medium-high heat. Add the pumpkin seeds, paprika, and the remaining 1 teaspoon of salt and season with pepper. Cook the pumpkin seeds, stirring and shaking the pan, until they are lightly toasted, 3 to 5 minutes. Set aside to cool.

Combine the rice, beans, and pumpkin seeds in a large bowl. Transfer half of the mixture to a food processor fitted with the metal blade and process until smooth, adding the reserved cooking liquid from the beans as needed to keep the mixture moist enough to stick together. Return the mixture to the bowl, mix everything together, and form patties about 3½ inches in diameter and 1 inch thick.

continued

To bake the burgers, preheat the oven to 350°F. Brush a baking sheet with olive oil and put the burgers on it. Brush the burgers with oil and bake until browned, 20 to 30 minutes, turning the burgers halfway through cooking. To pan-fry the burgers, coat a sauté pan with olive oil and heat the pan over medium heat. Add the burgers and cook for about 4 minutes per side.

To grill the onion slices, lightly brush with olive oil and sauté them in a sauté pan over medium-high heat, 2 minutes per side.

Serve the burgers on toasted burger rolls with the onion slices and avocado slices, if desired.

LaRocca Cabernet Sauvignon, California

Farming organically in Butte and Sutter Counties for twenty-six years, LaRocca makes full-flavored wines with no added sulfites. Their Cabernet Sauvignon, at home on many a backyard picnic table, is dry and rich, with cedar and spices on the finish that pair perfectly with smoky black bean burgers.

Sides, Sauces, and Secrets

Flavorful side dishes are as important as the main events in Candle 79's kitchen. Savory sautéed, roasted, and braised vegetables, along with inventively spiced and seasoned rice, grain, and noodle dishes, make great accompaniments to scores of recipes throughout the book. In addition, as we often do, numerous sides can be put together to make a meal.

Our sauces are also indispensable, adding an extra layer of flavor that can bring out the essence of a dish. Made with organic vegetables and herbs, fresh ginger, and a range of chiles and spices (among other good things), many of these sauces can be made well ahead of time and stored in the refrigerator so you'll have them on hand to create healthy and flavorful dishes at a moment's notice.

We consider the tasty and surprising combinations of flavors used in the side dishes and sauces in this chapter to be our restaurant's "secrets." These simple recipes always add an extra dimension of great taste to every plate that we serve—that magical element that elevates our food to the next level and always has customers asking, "How did you make this taste so good?"

Barbecued Black-Eyed Peas

This is a great go-to side dish that we serve in a number of ways. It's terrific with Tamarind-Barbecued Seitan (page 90)—and a great reuse for the leftover barbecue marinade. When Joy serves it at her summer barbecues, both kids and grown-ups alike devour it. Many other types of dried or canned beans work well with this recipe, so feel free to experiment. Note that dried beans must soak for at least 4 hours.

2 cups dried black-eyed peas, or
    2 (15-ounce) cans black-eyed
    peas, drained and rinsed
2 tablespoons extra-virgin olive oil
2 shallots, chopped
1 clove garlic, chopped
1¼ teaspoons sea salt
4 cups water
½ cup Tamarind Barbecue Sauce
    (page 90) or your favorite
    barbecue sauce
1 tablespoon chopped fresh flat-leaf
    parsley
1 tablespoon chopped fresh cilantro

Serves 4 to 6

If using dried black-eyed peas, put them in a large bowl and cover with cold water. Cover and let soak for at least 4 hours or overnight in the refrigerator. Drain and rinse.

Heat the olive oil in a soup pot over medium heat. Add the shallots and garlic and sauté until tender, 2 to 3 minutes. Add the black-eyed peas, salt, and water. Bring to a boil, then decrease the heat and simmer until the peas are just tender, 20 to 25 minutes. (If using canned black-eyed peas, you'll only need ½ cup of water, and the cooking time will be 5 to 10 minutes.) Drain the beans, reserving ½ cup of the liquid.

Add the barbecue sauce, parsley, and cilantro and cook, stirring occasionally, for 5 to 10 minutes, adding the reserved liquid to keep it moist. Taste and adjust the seasonings if necessary and serve warm.

Granny Smith Coleslaw

This simple summery slaw is a great picnic and summer side dish, and it's a snap to make. We also serve it on the side with our Tempeh Cakes (page 80). The Granny Smith apple gives it a pleasant crunch and sweetly nuanced flavor.

½ small white cabbage, shredded
1 carrot, cut into 1-inch julienne
2 Granny Smith apples, cored and
   cut into 1-inch julienne
3 tablespoons extra-virgin olive oil
3 tablespoons vegan mayonnaise
2 tablespoons freshly squeezed
   lemon juice
1 tablespoon chopped fresh flat-leaf
   parsley
¼ teaspoon sea salt
Pinch of freshly ground pepper

Serves 4 to 6

Put the cabbage, carrot, and apple in a large bowl.

In a small bowl, whisk together the oil, vegan mayo, lemon juice, parsley, salt, and pepper until well blended. Pour over the cabbage mixture and toss well. Taste and adjust the seasonings if necessary. Chill in the refrigerator for 1 or 2 hours before serving.

Sweet Potato Mash

This mash of sweet potatoes and cinnamon is a winner. We also add a bit of white miso to the mix, as it adds subtle hints of sweet and salty. We serve it as a side with a number of our entrées. If you want a smoother texture, process the potato mixture in a food processor after mashing. Either way is terrific!

3 pounds sweet potatoes
2 tablespoons grapeseed oil
¼ teaspoon ground cinnamon
1 tablespoon white miso
1 tablespoon Earth Balance Natural
   Buttery Spread

Serves 4 to 6

Preheat the oven to 350°F.

Wrap the sweet potatoes in aluminum foil. Roast the potatoes until fork-tender, 50 to 60 minutes. Remove and let cool.

Peel the potatoes, cut into 1-inch pieces, and transfer to a large bowl. Add the oil, cinnamon, miso, and buttery spread and mash well with a spoon or potato masher. Serve warm.

Roasted Fingerling Potatoes

We like to use a mix of fingerling potatoes in shades of yellow, rose, and purple for this simple, beautiful roast. We also add nutritional yeast—it has a nutty, cheesy taste that adds richness and another layer of flavor. If you can't find fingerlings, you can make this with any other type of potato, cut into wedges. This dish is great alongside almost anything.

1 pound fingerling potatoes,
    quartered lengthwise
3 tablespoons extra-virgin olive oil
1 tablespoon nutritional yeast
1 tablespoon chopped fresh flat-leaf
    parsley
Sea salt and freshly ground pepper

Serves 4 to 6

Preheat the oven to 350°F.

Put the potatoes in a bowl. In a small bowl, whisk together the oilve oil, nutritional yeast, and parsley, and season with salt and pepper. Pour the mixture over the potatoes and toss gently to coat.

Arrange the potatoes in a single layer on the baking sheet. Roast until tender and lightly browned, about 30 minutes.

Potato Cakes

Savory Potato Cakes are a staple in our kitchen. We serve them with Seitan Piccata (page 89) and as a breakfast side with our savory crepes (pages 131 and 133) and Tofu and Seitan Sausage Scramble (page 137).

1½ pounds Idaho potatoes, peeled and cut into ½-inch cubes
4 tablespoons extra-virgin olive oil
2 cups chopped white onions
1 tablespoon chopped fresh flat-leaf parsley
1 teaspoon sea salt
Pinch of freshly ground pepper

Serves 6 to 8

Bring a large pot of water to a boil over medium-high heat. Add the potatoes, decrease the heat slightly, and cook until tender, about 20 minutes. Drain the potatoes and transfer to a bowl.

Heat 2 tablespoons of the olive oil in a sauté pan over medium-high heat. Add the onions and sauté until soft and lightly browned, about 7 minutes.

Add the onions, parsley, salt, and pepper to the potatoes. Mash everything together with a spoon or potato masher.

Divide the mixture into 8 equal portions and flatten each into a cake about ½ inch thick. They should be about 3 inches in diameter.

Heat the remaining 2 tablespoons of olive oil in a large sauté pan over medium-high heat. Add the cakes and fry 3 minutes per side, until golden brown. Serve warm.

Polenta Fries

These fantastic fries are so popular at the restaurant, they seem to fly out of the kitchen! Just one taste of these "crunchy-on-the-outside, creamy-on-the-inside" fries and you'll be hooked too. They're terrific with all kinds of dishes, especially our Black Bean–Chipotle Burgers (page 95). For extra flavor, Joy often adds nutritional yeast to the polenta while it's cooking. If using quick-cooking polenta, cook it according to the package directions and then proceed with the recipe.

3 cups water
1 tablespoon chopped garlic
1 teaspoon sea salt
1½ cups fine yellow cornmeal
1 tablespoon chopped fresh flat-leaf
　parsley
½ cup safflower oil, plus more for
　oiling the pan

Serves 6

Lightly oil a 9 by 13-inch baking pan.

Put the water, garlic, and salt in a large saucepan, bring to a boil, and decrease the heat to medium-low. Pour the cornmeal through a sieve into the stock and whisk continuously to incorporate and avoid clumps.

Switch to a wooden spoon and continue stirring until the polenta begins to pull away from the sides of the pan, 10 to 15 minutes. If it becomes too dry to stick together, add ¼ cup of warm water. Fold in the parsley. Transfer the polenta to the prepared pan and spread it in an even layer. Let the polenta sit for at least 1 hour until it solidifies. The polenta can be refrigerated for up to 1 day at this point.

Cut the polenta into rectangles, rounds, or cubes.

In a deep cast-iron skillet, heat the oil over medium-high heat until hot but not smoking. There should be just enough oil to cover the polenta fries. Fry the polenta pieces, turning often, until crisp and golden on all sides. Remove the fries and drain on paper towels. Serve immediately.

Soba Noodles

Soba noodles are Japanese noodles made from buckwheat, some of which are all-buckwheat and therefore gluten free. Soba noodles are fun to experiment with. Joy loves to cook with kids, and she and her niece, Laura, developed a spicy rendition of this recipe. They turned up the heat by adding extra red pepper flakes. You can experiment with this recipe too, by tossing the noodles with your favorite vegetables, herbs, and spices. The possibilities are endless.

½ pound soba noodles
2 tablespoons grapeseed oil
¼ teaspoon sesame oil
¼ teaspoon chopped garlic
6 scallions, white and green parts,
    minced
2 tablespoons tamari
¾ to 1½ teaspoons red pepper flakes
1 tablespoon white sesame seeds

Serves 4 to 6

In a large pot, bring about 6 cups of water to a boil. Add the noodles and cook until tender, 6 to 8 minutes. Drain and rinse with cold water.

In a large sauté pan, heat the grapeseed and sesame oils over medium heat. Add the garlic and scallions and sauté for 2 minutes. Add the tamari, red pepper flakes, sesame seeds, and soba noodles. Cook, tossing constantly, for an additional 2 to 3 minutes, until well mixed. Serve warm.

Jasmine Rice

This fragrant side dish will fill your kitchen with fresh, exotic aromas. Jasmine rice, a long-grained variety that is grown primarily in Thailand, has a naturally nutty flavor that is enhanced when cooked with fresh herbs, ginger, and subtly sweet coconut milk. We love to serve this Asian-inspired delight with a variety of tofu and seitan dishes.

2 cups jasmine rice

3 cups water

¼ teaspoon chopped garlic

1 teaspoon finely chopped fresh ginger

1 teaspoon chopped fresh flat-leaf parsley

1 tablespoon minced fresh chives

2 bay leaves

¼ cup coconut milk

1 teaspoon sea salt

Serves 4 to 6

Rinse the rice under cold water for 30 seconds.

In a large saucepan over medium-high heat, bring the water to a boil, then add the rice. Stir in the garlic, ginger, parsley, chives, bay leaves, coconut milk, and salt, decrease the heat to medium-low, cover, and cook for 15 to 20 minutes. Remove from the heat and let sit, covered, for another 10 minutes before serving. Serve warm.

Quinoa-Vegetable Pilaf

Quinoa is an excellent source of protein with a slightly nutty flavor and fluffy, creamy texture. We like to cook it into a pilaf with mixed vegetables and serve it alongside our Chile-Grilled Tofu (page 76) or drizzled with Chipotle-Avocado dressing in our stuffed avocado salad (page 48).

2 cups water
1 cup quinoa
2 tablespoons extra-virgin olive oil
½ teaspoon sea salt, plus more for seasoning
1 tablespoon chopped fresh flat-leaf parsley
1 cup cooked fresh corn kernels
1 red bell pepper, seeded and cut into small dice
½ cup finely diced carrot
1 bunch scallions, white and green parts, chopped

Serves 4 to 6

Rinse the quinoa under cold water for 30 seconds. In a saucepan, bring the water to a boil. Add the quinoa, ½ teaspoon of the olive oil, and a pinch of salt and stir. Bring back to a boil, then decrease the heat and simmer, uncovered, for 10 minutes, stirring occasionally. Remove from the heat, cover, and let sit for 10 minutes.

Transfer the quinoa to a large bowl, stir in the parsley, and set aside.

Heat the remaining olive oil in a large sauté pan over medium heat. Add the corn, bell pepper, carrot, and the ½ teaspoon sea salt and sauté until the pepper is tender, about 7 minutes. Add the scallions and sauté for an additional 2 minutes.

Add the vegetables to the quinoa and toss gently until well combined. Serve warm or at room temperature.

Marinated Tempeh

This basic recipe for tempeh, which can be baked or grilled, is a solid foundation upon which you can build a number of savory, filling meals. At the restaurant, we use this in Tempeh Cakes (page 80), Stuffed Poblano Peppers (page 58), and Tempeh with Mole Sauce (page 83). Tempeh also makes a great salad topper, sandwich filler, or side dish.

½ cup tamari
2 cups water
1 tablespoon brown rice vinegar
1 tablespoon apple cider vinegar
1 clove garlic, chopped
⅓ cup chopped onion
3 bay leaves
1 lemongrass stalk, chopped
2 tablespoons safflower oil
1 pound tempeh, cut into 2-inch
    strips

Serves 4 to 6

In a large bowl, whisk together the tamari, water, vinegars, garlic, onion, bay leaves, lemongrass, and oil until well combined. Add the tempeh, cover, and let marinate in the refrigerator for 4 hours, stirring occasionally.

To bake the tempeh, preheat the oven to 350°F. Put the tempeh and marinade into a nonreactive baking dish. Bake the tempeh, turning once, until lightly browned, 20 to 30 minutes altogether. To grill the tempeh, prepare a medium-hot gas or charcoal grill. Grill the tempeh until golden brown, about 5 minutes per side.

Seitan Cutlets

These protein-packed cutlets are a great way to express the flavor of the season and the global versa-tility of vegan cuisine. Seitan is a perennial favorite with our guests—hardcore vegans and die-hard carnivores alike. Replace the meat with wheat, and we promise you'll never disappoint. This is the basic recipe for all of the seitan dishes in this book—the cutlets can be chopped or ground as needed. If you want to add an additional flavor to your seitan, you can cook it further in a flavored broth or marinade.

7 cups unbleached bread flour
3 cups whole wheat bread flour
4½ cups water
1½ teaspoons sea salt
8 cups vegetable stock or water
¼ cup tamari
1 piece of kombu
1 piece of wakame

Makes 6 to 8 cutlets, about 1½ pounds

Put the flours in a bowl. Mix the water and salt together and add to the flour. Stir until the mixture forms a ball of dough. When you have a nice ball, cover with water and let stand for 1 hour.

Pour off the water and rinse the dough under cold run-ning water until the water is almost clear. Divide the dough into 2 balls.

Put the stock in a large soup pot and bring to a boil. Add the tamari, kombu, and wakame and decrease the heat. Add the balls of dough and simmer, uncovered, for 2 hours, until they are firm and slice easily.

Drain the stock from the pot, reserving the stock if not using the seitan right away. Transfer the seitan to a bowl, add enough cold water to cover, and let sit for about 10 minutes.

Drain and slice the seitan into ½-inch-thick cutlets.

If not using the seitan at this point, store it (sliced or unsliced) in 4 cups of the reserved stock, covered, in the refrigerator for up to 1 month. Alternatively, the cutlets can be frozen (without the stock) for up to 3 months.

Sautéed Royal Trumpet Mushrooms

Royal trumpet, or Trumpet Royale, mushrooms are a favorite of our chefs because of their rich and nutty flavor, excellent texture, and versatility. They can be sautéed, braised, or grilled, and they pair well with any number of dishes. Here is our very simple sauté flavored with nothing more than a bit of olive oil, garlic, sea salt, and pepper. We recommend serving this with Pan-Seared Pine Nut Pesto Tofu (page 75).

3 tablespoons extra-virgin olive oil
2 cloves garlic, chopped
½ pound royal trumpet mushrooms, halved lengthwise
Sea salt and freshly ground pepper
1 tablespoon chopped fresh chives or flat-leaf parsley

Serves 4

Heat the oil in a sauté pan over medium heat, add the garlic, and sauté until softened, about 2 minutes. Add the mushrooms, season with salt and pepper, and cook, stirring occasionally, until the mushrooms are tender, 5 to 6 minutes. Garnish with the chives or parsley and serve.

Braised Green Beans

Vegetables that are slowly braised on the stovetop have a rich, mellow flavor. In this recipe, we cook green beans and shallots with vegetable stock over low heat until they are tender. This recipe works very well with larger pole beans too. We like to serve it alongside Tempeh with Mole Sauce (page 83).

2 tablespoons extra-virgin olive oil
2 shallots, thinly sliced
1 pound fresh green beans, trimmed
Sea salt and freshly ground pepper
½ to 1 cup vegetable stock
½ cup toasted slivered almonds

Serves 4 to 6

Heat the oil in a sauté pan over medium heat, add the shallots, and sauté until softened, about 3 minutes. Add the beans, season with salt and pepper, and cook, stirring occasionally, for 2 minutes.

Add a bit of the stock, decrease the heat to low, cover, and cook, stirring occasionally, until the stock is absorbed. Add more stock as needed, and continue cooking until the beans are very tender, 20 to 25 minutes. Sprinkle with the almonds, taste and adjust the seasonings if necessary, and serve warm.

Gingered Sugar Snap Peas

Look for garden-fresh sugar snap peas at your farmers' market in late spring and early summer. They are wonderful to eat raw for a snack or to cook in a simple sauté, like this one with shallots and ginger. In the restaurant we serve this dish with our Nori- and Sesame-Crusted Seitan (page 84).

1 pound sugar snap peas, trimmed
1 teaspoon grapeseed oil
¼ teaspoon toasted sesame oil
1 tablespoon chopped shallot
1 tablespoon finely chopped fresh
   ginger
Pinch of sea salt

Serves 4 to 6

Bring a pot of salted water to a boil. Add the peas and simmer for 2 minutes. Drain and rinse under cold water.

Heat the grapeseed and sesame oils in a sauté pan over medium heat. Add the shallot and ginger and sauté until softened, about 2 minutes. Add the peas and salt and sauté, stirring often, until just tender, 2 to 3 minutes.

Sautéed Swiss Chard

This simple preparation works with Swiss chard, as well as any other green or combination of greens. Chard is available in red, white, and rainbow varieties. This is excellent with Tamarind-Barbecued Seitan (page 90) and Stuffed Poblano Peppers (page 58).

3 tablespoons extra-virgin olive oil
2 tablespoons chopped shallot
1 clove garlic, thinly sliced
1 pound Swiss chard, leaves and
    stems separated
Sea salt and freshly ground pepper

Serves 4

Heat the oil in a sauté pan over medium heat, add the shallot and garlic, and sauté for 1 minute. Add the chard stems, season with salt and pepper, cover, and cook, stirring occasionally, until tender, 3 to 5 minutes. Add the leaves and cook, stirring occasionally, until the chard is just wilted, about 3 minutes. Serve warm.

Creamed Spinach

Candle 79's creamed spinach, made with silken tofu and vegan mayo, is a delicious alternative to the high-fat version that traditionally uses heavy cream and cheese. This classic side dish pairs well with our Seitan Piccata (page 89) and is also good to serve for the holidays.

2 pounds fresh spinach, tough stems removed
1 cup coarsely chopped silken tofu
½ cup vegan mayonnaise
½ teaspoon minced garlic
1 tablespoon chopped fresh flat-leaf parsley
1 tablespoon freshly squeezed lemon juice
1 tablespoon extra-virgin olive oil
1 teaspoon sea salt
½ teaspoon freshly ground pepper

Serves 4 to 6

Bring a pot of salted water to a boil over high heat. Add the spinach and cook for 2 minutes.

Drain in a fine-mesh strainer, pressing with a large spoon to release as much water as possible. Finely chop the spinach and transfer to a large bowl.

Put the tofu, vegan mayo, garlic, parsley, lemon juice, olive oil, salt, and pepper in a blender or food processor fitted with the metal blade and process until smooth.

Pour the mixture into a medium saucepan and gently cook over medium-low heat, making sure the mixture doesn't boil. Once the mixture is warmed through, remove from the heat. Pour it over the spinach and gently mix together. Taste and adjust the seasonings if necessary. Serve warm.

Ginger-Soy Dipping Sauce

Here's a fantastic sauce that we serve with our Ginger-Seitan Dumplings (page 23). It's also delicious drizzled over vegetables and as a salad dressing. Keep it handy in the refrigerator for a quick lift to so many dishes.

2 tablespoons grapeseed oil
¼ cup water
¼ cup brown rice vinegar
1 tablespoon sesame oil
2 teaspoons tamari
2 teaspoons agave nectar
1½ teaspoons ginger juice
2 teaspoons finely chopped garlic
1 teaspoon grated fresh ginger
1 teaspoon finely chopped scallions, white and green parts
1 teaspoon finely chopped fresh cilantro
½ teaspoon red pepper flakes

Makes about 1¼ cups

In bowl, whisk together all the ingredients until well mixed. For a more integrated dipping sauce, use a blender.

This sauce will keep, covered, in the refrigerator for up to 1 month.

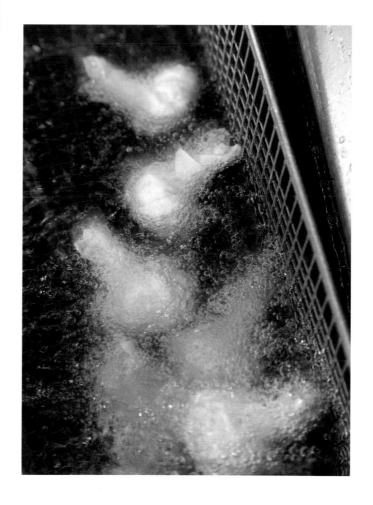

Roasted Plum Tomato Sauce

This tomato sauce is a kitchen staple at Candle 79. It can be made well ahead of time and it freezes beautifully, so you can always have it on hand to use in a variety of dishes. We serve it with arancini (page 15), and it's terrific with pasta or Polenta Fries (page 104).

12 ripe plum tomatoes, seeded and halved, or 1 (28-ounce) can plum tomatoes, drained and juices reserved
2 tablespoons extra-virgin olive oil
2 tablespoons Earth Balance Natural Buttery Spread
½ cup chopped onion
2 tablespoons chopped fresh basil leaves
½ cup water
Sea salt and freshly ground pepper

Makes about 2½ cups

Preheat the oven to 350°F.

Put the tomatoes on a rimmed baking sheet, drizzle with the olive oil, and roast for 30 minutes. Let cool, then chop coarsely.

Heat the buttery spread in a large sauté pan over medium heat. Add the onion and sauté until softened, about 5 minutes. Stir in the tomatoes, basil, water, and salt and pepper to taste, and cook over low heat for 15 to 20 minutes. If using canned tomatoes, add the reserved juices to the sauce before cooking. The sauce should be fairly chunky, but if you prefer a thinner sauce, add a bit of vegetable stock, transfer to a blender, and process until smooth.

This sauce will keep, covered, in the refrigerator for up to 1 week.

Red Bell Pepper–Curry Sauce

We serve this spicy sauce with Morrocan-Spiced Chickpea Cakes (page 66). It's also very good with grilled tofu or drizzled over basmati or jasmine rice.

3 red bell peppers
1 tablespoon extra-virgin olive oil,
    plus more for brushing
¼ cup grapeseed oil
½ cup chopped onion
1 cup coconut milk
1 teaspoon curry powder
1 teaspoon ground cumin
1 teaspoon sea salt
3 tablespoons tomato paste
¼ cup chopped fresh cilantro

Makes about 2 cups

Preheat the oven to 350°F.

Arrange the peppers on a rimmed baking sheet and drizzle with the olive oil. Roast until tender, about 40 minutes. Transfer to a bowl, cover with plastic wrap, and let sit for about 10 minutes. When cool enough to handle, peel and chop the peppers.

Heat the grapeseed oil in a sauté pan over medium heat. Add the onion and sauté until softened, about 5 minutes. Let cool. Put the peppers, onion, coconut milk, curry powder, cumin, salt, tomato paste, and cilantro in a blender and process until smooth.

Transfer the mixture back to the pan and cook over medium heat, stirring occasionally, until thickened, 10 to 15 minutes. Serve right away, or reheat just before serving.

The sauce will keep, covered, in the refrigerator for up to 1 week.

Roasted Red Bell Pepper and Tomato Sauce

We love the deep, rich flavor of smoked paprika, or pimenton, and we use it in a number of recipes for soups, stews, and sauces, including this luscious sauce made with roasted bell peppers and fresh tomatoes. It's a very good accompaniment to Stuffed Poblano Peppers (page 58). You can also try it with Potato Gnocci (page 73) or Saffron Ravioli (page 69).

2 red bell peppers
4 tomatoes
3 tablespoons extra-virgin olive oil
½ cup chopped onion
1 clove garlic
½ teaspoon smoked paprika
1 teaspoon sea salt
2 cups vegetable stock

Makes about 2 cups

Preheat the oven to 350°F.

Put the peppers and tomatoes on rimmed baking sheets and drizzle with 2 tablespoons of the olive oil. Roast until tender, about 30 minutes. Transfer to a large bowl, cover with plastic wrap, and let cool. Peel and chop the peppers and tomatoes.

Heat the remaining tablespoon of olive oil in a large saucepan over medium heat. Add the onion and garlic and sauté for 2 minutes. Add the paprika, salt, stock, and roasted peppers and tomatoes and cook over medium-low heat, stirring occasionally, for 15 to 20 minutes. Remove from the heat and let cool a bit.

Transfer to a blender and process until smooth. Taste and adjust the seasonings if necessary.

This sauce will keep, covered, in the refrigerator for up to 1 week.

Mint-Cilantro Chimichurri Sauce

There are many ways to make the Argentinian classic, chimichurri sauce. The main components of the sauce are usually chopped parsley, olive oil, onions, and garlic. Our version is made with fresh cilantro, mint, and jalapeño peppers. Its sweet and spicy taste is the perfect complement to Cashew Cheese–Stuffed Yuca Cakes (page 18). It's also great over Jasmine Rice (page 106) or steamed quinoa.

⅓ cup white wine vinegar
½ cup extra-virgin olive oil
1 cup finely chopped fresh cilantro
½ cup finely chopped fresh mint
    leaves
5 cloves garlic, finely chopped
2 jalapeño peppers, seeded and
    finely chopped
Sea salt and freshly ground pepper

Makes about 1 cup

    In a medium bowl, whisk together the vinegar and olive oil until well combined. Stir in the cilantro, mint, garlic, and jalapeño peppers. Add salt and pepper to taste and whisk again.

    This sauce will keep, covered, in the refrigerator for up to 1 week.

Pesto

A pesto based on fresh basil and pine nuts is now as commonplace as tomato sauce, but this versatile sauce can also be made with other fresh herbs and greens, such as cilantro, mint, and arugula. We also use walnuts, pecans, and cashews, as well as the traditional pine nuts. No matter how you make pesto, it's fabulous with pasta, spread on a sandwich or pizza, or drizzled over grilled vegetables or roasted potatoes.

1 cup chopped fresh basil leaves
1 cup chopped fresh flat-leaf parsley
1 clove garlic, thinly sliced
1 cup pine nuts
1 teaspoon freshly squeezed lemon juice
2 tablespoons nutritional yeast
2 to 3 tablespoons extra-virgin olive oil
Salt and freshly ground pepper

Makes about 2 cups

Put the basil, parsley, garlic, nuts, lemon juice, and nutritional yeast in a food processor fitted with the metal blade. With the motor running, drizzle the olive oil through the feed tube and process until the mixture is pureed. Add salt and pepper to taste.

Transfer to a bowl and cover tightly. Refrigerate, covered, until ready to use. The pesto will keep in the refrigerator for 2 to 3 days. Bring to room temperature before using.

Zucchini Blossom Sauce

We are big fans of zucchini blossoms, the young flowers that bloom on zucchini plants. They begin to appear in early summer and their growing season usually lasts through the summer. If you don't grow zucchini in your garden, you can probably find the blossoms in supermarkets and farmers' markets in season. In addition to Zucchini Blossom Tempura (page 12), we use these delicate blossoms to make this sauce, which is terrific with Tempeh Cakes (page 80).

2 tablespoons extra-virgin olive oil
½ white onion, chopped
2 small cloves garlic, chopped
10 zucchini blossoms, trimmed and
    small leaves removed
2 tablespoons chopped fresh cilantro
2 cups vegetable stock
1 teaspoon sea salt

Makes about 3 cups

Heat the olive oil in a large saucepan over medium heat. Add the onion and garlic and sauté until softened, 2 to 3 minutes. Stir in the zucchini blossoms, cilantro, stock, and salt, decrease the heat, and simmer for 15 minutes. Remove from the heat and let cool a bit.

Transfer the mixture to a blender and process until smooth. The sauce will keep, covered, in the refrigerator for up to 3 days.

Edamame-Mint Sauce

Nutty, delicious edamame—green soybeans in a pod—are often served as a snack in Asian restaurants. High in protein and fiber, edamame make a light and lovely sauce when blended with fresh scallions and mint. We serve this beautiful green sauce with Nori- and Sesame-Crusted Seitan (page 84). You can also try it over your favorite salads or grains.

2 tablespoons extra-virgin olive oil
1 cup chopped scallions, white and
    green parts
1 cup shelled edamame
1 clove garlic, chopped
1 jalapeño pepper, seeded and
    chopped
1 teaspoon sea salt
2 cups water
½ cup chopped fresh mint leaves

Makes about 2 cups

Heat the olive oil in a saucepan over medium heat. Add the scallions and sauté until softened, 1 to 2 minutes. Add the edamame, garlic, jalapeño pepper, salt, and water and cook, stirring occasionally, for 10 to 15 minutes. Add the mint, remove from the heat, and let cool a bit.

Transfer the mixture to a blender and process until smooth. The sauce will keep, covered, in the refrigerator for up to 3 days.

Apricot Chutney

Fresh apricots have a short growing season and are usually available in early summer. A dollop of this chutney is wonderful over Moroccan-Spiced Chickpea Cakes (page 66). It also makes a great spread over naan or paratha bread, alongside Smoked Paprika Hummus (page 17).

3 tablespoons grapeseed oil
½ cup chopped onion
2 tablespoons chopped fresh ginger
3 cups chopped fresh apricots
¼ teaspoon sea salt
2 tablespoons agave nectar
½ cup water

Makes about 2 cups

Heat the oil in a large saucepan over medium heat. Add the onion and sauté until softened, about 3 minutes. Add the ginger, apricots, salt, agave nectar, and water. Cover and cook over low heat, stirring occasionally, until thickened, about 20 minutes. The chutney will keep, covered, in the refrigerator for up to 2 weeks.

Cashew Crème Fraîche

We use cashews that are soaked, drained, and blended in a number of our dishes. Here we make a vegan version of crème fraîche, sans cream. It makes a delicious garnish for Seitan Cakes (page 20) as well as soups, potato dishes, and roasted vegetables. Note that the cashews must soak overnight before using.

2 cups raw cashews
¼ cup freshly squeezed lemon juice
2 tablespoons extra-virgin olive oil
¾ cup water
½ teaspoon sea salt

Makes about 2 cups

Put the cashews in a bowl and add enough cold water to cover them. Cover and let soak overnight in the refrigerator.

Drain the cashews, rinse under cold water, and drain again.

Transfer to a blender. Add the lemon juice, olive oil, water, and salt and process until smooth. The mixture will keep, covered, in the refrigerator for up to 5 days.

Sage or Tarragon Aioli

Aioli is a gutsy and garlicky mayonnaise that makes a perfect spread for sandwiches and great topper for hors d'oeuvres and other dishes. Sage and tarragon are two of our most popular herb-infused varieties. We serve the tarragon aioli on our Wild Mushroom, Asparagus, and Spring Vegetable Crepes (page 131) and Cashew Cheese–Stuffed Yuca Cakes (page 18), and the sage aioli is an ideal match for the Butternut Squash, Mushroom, and Sage Crepes (page 133). Use this recipe to experiment with your favorite herbs and spices to find out what works best for your palate. Unleash your inner chef!

1½ tablespoons extra-virgin olive oil
3 cloves garlic, chopped
3 fresh sage leaves or 4 teaspoons
    chopped fresh tarragon
½ cup vegan mayonnaise
¼ cup soy milk
1 teaspoon freshly squeezed lemon
    juice
½ teaspoon chopped fresh flat-leaf
    parsley
Pinch of sea salt
Pinch of freshly ground pepper

Makes about 1 cup

Heat the olive oil in a small sauté pan over medium heat. Add the garlic and sauté for 3 minutes.

Combine the sage, vegan mayo, soy milk, lemon juice, parsley, salt, and pepper in a blender and process until smooth. Add the garlic and oil and blend until well combined.

The aioli will keep, covered, in the refrigerator for up to 2 weeks.

Brunch

We think that weekend brunch should be a relaxing and leisurely affair to enjoy while sipping coffee or tea and reading the paper. What could be more pleasant than whipping up warm and homey dishes like Sourdough French Toast (page 136), Home-Style Pancakes with Blueberry Butter (page 134), or a fluffy Tofu and Seitan Sausage Scramble (page 137)? This chapter has a delightful array of brunch favorites from the restaurant for you to make at home. It's soul-warming comfort food that's good for you and also fun and easy to prepare for you and your family, or a houseful of weekend guests.

Chickpea Crepes

This delicious, wheat- and gluten-free recipe is great for savory brunch crepes—we stuff them with sautéed seasonal vegetables and wild mushrooms.

1 cup soy milk
½ cup chickpea flour
2 tablespoons arrowroot powder
¼ teaspoon sea salt
¼ teaspoon finely chopped fresh
    flat-leaf parsley
½ teaspoon finely chopped fresh
    chives

Makes 6 crepes

Put the soy milk, chickpea flour, arrowroot powder, and salt in a blender and process until smooth. Transfer to a bowl. Add the parsley and chives and mix well.

Spray a medium nonstick skillet or crepe pan with olive oil cooking spray (or brush with olive oil), heat the pan over medium heat, and then pour about ¼ cup of the batter into the center of the pan. Quickly lift the pan off the heat and tip it in several directions so the batter covers the bottom of the pan.

Return the pan to the heat and cook for 2 to 3 minutes, or until the edges of the crepe begin to brown. Using a spatula, flip the crepe and cook for about 1 minute, until lightly browned. Transfer the crepe to a plate. Continue cooking crepes with the remaining batter, adding more cooking spray if needed, and stacking them on top of each other as they are cooked.

Wild Mushroom, Asparagus, and Spring Vegetable Crepes

With a filling of savory mushrooms, fresh and tender peas, fava beans, and asparagus, there is spring in every bite of these elegant crepes. There is no better or more delicious way to welcome the season.

½ cup shelled fava beans
2 tablespoons extra-virgin olive oil
1 cup chopped leek, white and pale green parts
1 pound morel mushrooms or oyster mushrooms, or a combination, trimmed and sliced
1 teaspoon sea salt
Pinch of freshly ground pepper
½ cup shelled fresh green peas
1 cup trimmed and sliced fresh asparagus

6 Chickpea Crepes (Page 130)
½ cup Tarragon Aioli (page 126)

Serves 6

Bring a pot of salted water to a boil. Add the fava beans and cook until tender, 3 to 4 minutes. Drain and rinse under cold water. Drain again thoroughly, then peel or pinch off the thin outer skins.

Heat the olive oil in a sauté pan over medium heat. Add the leek, and sauté over medium heat for 2 minutes. Add the mushrooms, salt, and pepper and sauté until the mushrooms are slightly softened, about 5 minutes. Add the peas, fava beans, and asparagus and sauté until softened, 3 to 5 minutes.

To serve, put 1 crepe in the center of a plate, spoon one-sixth of the vegetable mixture onto one side of the crepe, and fold the other side over the filling. Repeat with the remaining crepes and filling and serve with a dollop of aioli.

Butternut Squash, Mushroom, and Sage Crepes

There is no better time of year than autumn in New York. The air is crisp, and earthy produce fills the bins at farmers' markets. On weekends, we serve a number of brunch dishes through the afternoon, and one of the most popular is this seasonal crepe that speaks of fall.

2 cups peeled, diced butternut
    squash
2 tablespoons extra-virgin olive oil
½ cup chopped onion
1½ pounds cremini mushrooms,
    stemmed and thinly sliced
1 tablespoon chopped fresh sage
1 teaspoon sea salt

6 Chickpea Crepes (page 130)
½ cup Sage Aioli (page 126)
Chopped fresh chives, for garnish

Serves 6

Preheat the oven to 350°F.

Put the squash in a bowl with 1 tablespoon of the olive oil. Toss well to coat, then transfer to a rimmed baking sheet. Roast the squash until tender, 20 to 30 minutes.

Heat the remaining tablespoon of olive oil in a sauté pan over medium-low heat. Add the onion and sauté until caramelized, 8 to 10 minutes. Add the mushrooms and sauté until their liquid has evaporated, 8 to 10 minutes. Stir in the sage, salt, and squash and cook for about 2 minutes.

To serve, put 1 crepe in the center of a plate, spoon one-sixth of the vegetable mixture onto one side of the crepe, and fold the other side over the filling. Repeat with the remaining crepes and filling. Serve with a dollop of aioli and a scattering of chives.

Home-Style Pancakes with Blueberry Butter

This breakfast sensation will appeal to kids and adults alike. You'll probably end up with extra blueberry butter, which is great to have on hand in the fridge for spreading on toast or over oatmeal. We recommend using Earth Balance spread, which is made from a combination of vegetable oils and has a smooth, buttery texture. It is available at natural food stores and in the dairy section of many supermarkets.

Blueberry Butter
1 cup Earth Balance Natural Buttery
    Spread, softened
½ cup fresh blueberries

1½ cups unbleached all-purpose
    flour
2 tablespoons baking powder
¼ cup sugar
1 teaspoon sea salt
1 teaspoon ground cinnamon
1 tablespoon Ener-G egg replacer
2 cups soy milk
¼ cup Earth Balance Natural
    Buttery Spread, melted
1 teaspoon vanilla extract
Fresh fruit, for accompaniment
Maple syrup, for accompaniment

Serves 4 to 6; makes about 12 pancakes

To make the fruit butter, put the buttery spread in a blender. Add the blueberries and process until well incorporated. Store in the refrigerator until ready to serve.

Put the flour, baking powder, sugar, salt, cinnamon, and egg replacer in a large bowl and stir to combine. In another bowl, whisk together the soy milk, melted buttery spread, and vanilla and add to the flour mixture. Stir until just combined.

Spray a large nonstick sauté pan with canola oil cooking spray and heat the pan over medium heat. Drop large spoonfuls of batter into the pan, leaving room for the pancakes to expand. Cook until the bottoms are golden and bubbles are popping to the surface, 1 or 2 minutes. Flip the pancakes and cook the second side until golden. Repeat with the remaining batter. Serve with the fruit butter, fresh fruit, and maple syrup.

Sourdough French Toast

Thick slices of moist sourdough bread laced with autumnal spices and then fried make a sublime breakfast. This French toast is a great start to any day, and we especially love to make it for family and friends on holiday mornings. Tofu cream cheese is a cholesterol- and dairy-free alternative to everyone's favorite bagel spread; we recommend Galaxy or Toffuti.

1 cup tofu cream cheese
1 cup soy milk
⅓ cup maple syrup
1-inch piece of fresh ginger, peeled and finely grated
1 tablespoon granulated sugar
¼ teaspoon ground cardamom
½ teaspoon ground cinnamon
½ teaspoon ground or freshly grated nutmeg
2 tablespoons safflower oil, plus more for cooking
1 loaf sourdough bread, sliced into 1-inch-thick pieces
Maple syrup, confectioners' sugar, or fresh fruit, for accompaniment

Serves 4 to 6

Put the cream cheese, soy milk, maple syrup, ginger, sugar, cardamom, cinnamon, nutmeg, and oil in a blender and process until smooth. Transfer the mixture to a large bowl.

Brush a large nonstick sauté pan with oil and heat the pan over medium heat. Dip the bread slices into the soy milk mixture, then shake off any excess. Place a couple of dipped bread slices in the pan and cook until golden brown, 1 to 2 minutes per side. Serve with maple syrup, confectioners' sugar, or fresh fruit.

Tofu and Seitan Sausage Scramble

We love to whip up this hearty and soul-satisfying scramble on lazy weekend mornings. It's terrific with golden Potato Cakes (page 103) and whole-grain toast. We also use it to make a filling breakfast burrito with black beans, salsa, and guacamole. We recommend seitan sausages from Field Roast Grain Meat Co. (see Resources, page 182).

1½ pounds extra-firm tofu
2 tablespoons extra-virgin olive oil
1 cup chopped onion
1 clove garlic, chopped
2 cups diced fresh or canned tomatoes
½ cup vegetable stock
1 teaspoon sea salt
2 jalapeño peppers, seeded and diced
½ cup diced or crumbled seitan sausage
2 tablespoons nutritional yeast
1 tablespoon Earth Balance Natural Buttery Spread
2 tablespoons chopped fresh cilantro
1 cup chopped fresh spinach

Serves 4 to 6

With clean hands, crumble the tofu. Transfer to a colander to drain.

Heat the oil in a large sauté pan over medium heat for 1 minute. Add the onion, garlic, tomatoes, stock, salt, and tofu. Stir everything together, then cover and cook for 4 minutes. Stir in the jalapeño peppers, sausage, nutritional yeast, buttery spread, and cilantro and cook, stirring occasionally, for 5 minutes. Add the spinach and cook for another minute. Taste and adjust the seasonings if necessary. Serve at once.

Mixed-Grain Waffles with Raspberry Butter

Heat your waffle iron and whip up a batch of these yummy waffles for the whole family. You can substitute other berries for raspberries to change the flavor of the fruit butter (of which you'll have extra for toast or other uses). We also like to top these waffles with sliced fruit, fresh berries, and maple syrup.

Raspberry Butter
1 cup Earth Balance Natural Buttery
    Spread, softened
½ cup fresh raspberries

2 teaspoons flaxseeds
1 cup unbleached all-purpose flour
¾ cup whole wheat pastry flour
1 tablespoon baking powder
2 tablespoons sugar
2 teaspoons Ener-G egg replacer
½ teaspoon sea salt
1 teaspoon ground cinnamon
¼ teaspoon ground or freshly grated
    nutmeg
½ cup sparkling water
1½ cups soy milk
1½ teaspoons vanilla extract
2 tablespoons Earth Balance Natural
    Buttery Spread, melted
Maple syrup, sliced fruit, or berries,
    for accompaniment

Serves 6

To make the fruit butter, put the buttery spread in a blender. Add the raspberries and process until well incorporated. Store in the refrigerator until ready to serve.

Spray a waffle iron with canola oil cooking spray and heat according to the manufacturer's instructions.

Put the flaxseeds in a blender and process until pulverized.

In a large bowl, combine the flours, baking powder, sugar, egg replacer, salt, cinnamon, nutmeg, and ground flaxseeds. In a small bowl, whisk together the sparkling water and soy milk. Add the vanilla extract and buttery spread and whisk again.

Add the wet ingredients to the dry ingredients and stir just until combined, being careful not to overmix.

Cook the batter in the prepared waffle iron until golden brown, about 4 to 5 minutes. Serve with the fruit butter, along with maple syrup, sliced fruit, or berries, as desired.

Desserts

When it comes to dessert, our motto is "Always save the best for last." Candle 79 is famous for its rich, delicious desserts, and our customers are always amazed that we use no dairy products or refined sugars in our baking and dessert making. Instead, we make our creations with organic ingredients such as silken and firm tofu, soy milk, unrefined sugar, agave nectar, maple syrup, and natural fruit juices. Luckily for the home cook, these items are increasingly available at mainstream supermarkets, as well as natural food stores and online outlets—see Resources for more information.

Whether you have a craving for chocolate, berries, or sweet spices, we know that you will enjoy whipping up these luscious and luxurious desserts for all occasions!

Summer Berry Crumble

Take full advantage of bursting-with-flavor fresh berries in season and make this fantastic berry crumble—a perfect ending to any summer meal. We add almond flour to the crumble, which contributes great flavor and moistness. Almond flour, made from blanched almonds, has a cornmeal-like consistency and is a good addition to many baked goods like muffins and quick breads. It is available at natural food stores and online. For extra indulgence, serve with a scoop of vegan Vanilla Bean Ice Cream (page 144).

Almond Crumble

1¼ cups Earth Balance Natural Buttery Spread, at room temperature
¼ cup unrefined sugar
1¾ cups unbleached all-purpose flour
1 cup almond flour
½ cup arrowroot powder

Almond Topping

1 tablespoon unrefined sugar
2 cups slivered almonds
¼ cup maple syrup

Strawberry Sauce

2 cups fresh strawberries, stemmed
¼ cup agave nectar
1 whole vanilla bean or 1 teaspoon vanilla extract

1 cup fresh strawberries, sliced, plus whole strawberries for garnish
1 cup fresh raspberries
1 cup fresh blueberries
1 cup fresh blackberries

Serves 6 to 8

To make the crumble, in a large bowl mix the buttery spread and sugar together with your hands. Add the all-purpose flour, almond flour, and arrowroot powder and continue mixing until everything is well blended. Cover and let chill in the refrigerator for 1 hour.

Preheat the oven to 350°F. Line 2 rimmed baking sheets with parchment paper.

Crumble the dough over one of the prepared baking sheets and bake for 20 minutes, turning with a spatula after 10 minutes, until golden brown. Remove and let cool.

To make the topping, put the sugar, almonds, and maple syrup in a bowl and stir with a spoon or mix very well with your hands. Spread the mixture evenly on the second baking sheet and bake for 8 to 12 minutes, until toasted.

To make the sauce, put the strawberries, agave nectar, and vanilla bean in a blender and process until smooth and creamy.

Gently stir the strawberries, raspberries, blueberries, and blackberries together.

To assemble each serving, spoon some sauce on the bottom of a dessert plate or shallow bowl. Add some almond crumble and a handful of mixed berries, then sprinkle with the topping. Garnish with a strawberry and serve.

Vanilla Bean Ice Cream

This vegan ice cream is made with soy milk, soy creamer, and coconut milk, which adds a rich, naturally sweet flavor. It is wonderful to eat on its own, but you can design your own flavors by adding your favorite fresh berries, chopped fresh fruit, or a handful of chocolate chips to the ice cream. Check the directions that accompany your ice cream maker as to when to add the mix-ins.

1 cup soy milk
1 cup soy creamer
¼ cup safflower oil
1 whole vanilla bean
½ cup unrefined sugar
2 cups coconut milk
2 cups fresh strawberries,
   blueberries, or blackberries; or
   3 cups chopped fresh fruit
   (such as peaches, bananas,
   or mangoes); or ½ cup vegan
   semisweet chocolate chips
   (optional)

Makes about 1½ quarts

Put the soy milk, soy creamer, safflower oil, vanilla bean, sugar, and coconut milk in a blender and process for 1 minute. Strain the mixture through a fine-mesh sieve to remove any pieces of vanilla bean.

Add any desired mix-ins and stir them in. Transfer the mixture to an ice cream maker and freeze according to the manufacturer's instructions.

Chocolate Ice Cream

Creamy, rich, and delicious chocolate ice cream is always a treat. No one can believe that this recipe is dairy free. You can find soy creamer in the refrigerated section of your local grocery store.

1 cup soy milk
¼ cup maple syrup
¾ cup vegan semisweet chocolate
  chips
1 cup coconut milk
1 cup soy creamer
½ cup safflower oil
1 cup unrefined sugar
1 whole vanilla bean

Makes about 1½ quarts

To make the chocolate sauce base, put ½ cup of the soy milk in a saucepan and cook over medium heat until very hot but not boiling. Stir in the maple syrup and chocolate chips and transfer the mixture to a blender. Blend until smooth, then let cool in the blender.

To complete the ice cream mixture, add the coconut milk, soy creamer, safflower oil, sugar, vanilla bean, and the remaining ½ cup soy milk to the blender and blend until smooth, about 1 minute. Strain the mixture through a fine-mesh sieve to remove any pieces of vanilla bean.

Transfer the mixture to an ice cream maker and freeze according to the manufacturer's instructions.

Sorbets

Sorbets made with fresh berries and fruit are very easy to whip up for light and refreshing desserts. Using seasonal, organic fruits is a great way to get deep flavor with natural sweetness. It's worth the extra effort to make several flavors and serve them together in shallow bowls or on dessert plates, as we've done (opposite, with mango and strawberry sorbets alongside a couple ice creams). They taste as beautiful as they look.

3 cups fresh berries (such as strawberries, blueberries, or blackberries), or 3 cups chopped fresh fruit (such as peaches, bananas, or mangoes)
¼ cup agave nectar
1 teaspoon safflower oil
1 cup water

Makes 1¹/₂ quarts

In a large bowl, mix together the fruit, agave nectar, safflower oil, and water. Transfer to a blender and process for 3 minutes. Taste and adjust the sweetness with additional agave nectar, if necessary.

Transfer the mixture in an ice cream maker and freeze according to the manufacturer's instructions.

Mexican Chocolate Cake

Our chocolate cake is memorable. It's beautifully spiced with cinnamon, and ancho chile powder gives it a subtle, unexpected kick. Our customers are mad for it!

1 cup unbleached all-purpose flour
½ cup cocoa powder
¾ teaspoon baking powder
⅛ teaspoon ground cinnamon
⅛ teaspoon ancho chile powder
⅛ teaspoon baking soda
1 cup soy milk
½ cup maple syrup
½ cup safflower oil
¼ cup unrefined sugar
1 teaspoon apple cider vinegar

Chocolate Sauce
1 cup soy milk
½ cup maple syrup
1½ cups vegan semisweet chocolate
    chips

Makes two 9-inch cakes or 12 cupcakes

Preheat the oven to 350°F. Brush two 9-inch round cake pans with safflower oil and set aside. If making cupcakes, brush a 12-cup muffin pan with safflower oil or line with cupcake papers.

In a large bowl, combine the flour, cocoa, baking powder, cinnamon, ancho powder, and baking soda and mix well. In a separate bowl, combine the soy milk, maple syrup, safflower oil, sugar, and vinegar and mix well.

Add the wet ingredients to the dry ingredients and stir to combine.

Divide the batter between the prepared pans and bake for 35 minutes, until a cake tester comes out clean. Cool in the pans on wire racks.

Meanwhile, to make the sauce, heat the soy milk in a saucepan over medium heat until very warm but not boiling. Transfer to a blender. Add the maple syrup and chocolate chips and blend until smooth.

Cut the cakes into wedges, drizzle with sauce, and serve.

Apple-Apricot Strudel

Apricot jam makes this strudel extra luscious, but during the summer you can make this with fresh stone fruits. Fall is the perfect time to feature apples, and this also makes a great holiday dessert. The phyllo is light and crunchy and is a perfect complement to an ice cream topping. A piece of this strudel, fresh from the oven and topped with a scoop of Vanilla Bean Ice Cream (page 144), is a slice of heaven.

¼ cup plus 1 tablespoon Earth
    Balance Natural Buttery Spread
¼ cup agave nectar
3 tart apples, such as Granny Smith,
    peeled, cored, and cut into
    ¼-inch slices
2 tablespoons unrefined sugar
1½-inch piece of vanilla bean
3 sheets phyllo dough
¼ cup apricot jam

Serves 6 to 8

Preheat oven to 375°F. Grease a baking sheet.

In a small saucepan, melt the ¼ cup buttery spread over medium heat. Add the agave nectar and stir well. Remove from the heat.

In a bowl, toss together the apples, sugar, and 1 tablespoon buttery spread. Split the vanilla bean lengthwise with a paring knife, scrape the seeds into the bowl, and stir to combine.

Place a sheet of phyllo dough on a work surface with a long side facing you. Brush the dough with some of the agave nectar mixture and place another sheet on top. Brush and layer the remaining sheets of phyllo dough, reserving a bit of the agave nectar mixture.

Spread the jam down the center of the phyllo, parallel to the longer side. Top with the apple mixture. Lift the long edge over the fruit and roll it over, leaving the seam side down. Brush the surface of the roll with the remaining agave nectar mixture.

Transfer the roll to the baking sheet, seam side down, and bake until the crust is golden brown and the apple mixture is bubbling, about 30 minutes.

Let cool for about 30 minutes, then slice and serve warm.

Peach Parfait

Peaches are the perfect succulent expression of summer. This parfait is a light and luscious way to end a great meal—especially when topped with a scoop of your favorite fruit sorbet (page 146). For more variety, replace the peaches in this recipe with other summer fruit. We like to make a parfait with fresh cherries and a cherry port reduction. Make extra granola and you have a wonderful breakfast cereal. If you have a dehydrator, you can use it instead of the oven for baking the granola. Note that the cashews must soak overnight before using.

Vanilla Cashew Cream

1 cup raw cashews
1 cup baby Thai coconut meat, or
    ½ cup creamed coconut
1 teaspoon coconut oil
1 tablespoon agave nectar
1½-inch piece of vanilla bean

Nut Granola

¾ cup dates
¼ cup raisins
2 tablespoons maple syrup
1 teaspoon vanilla extract
Pinch of sea salt
¼ teaspoon grated orange zest
¼ teaspoon freshly squeezed orange
    juice
1 cup raw cashews
½ cup raw sunflower seeds
1 cup sliced raw almonds
1 cup raw pecan pieces
¼ cup raw pumpkin seeds
½ cup shredded coconut

Peach Topping

4 cups peeled, diced fresh peaches
½ cup agave nectar
¼ cup freshly squeezed orange juice
1-inch piece of vanilla bean

Serves 4 to 6

To make the cashew cream, the day before serving, put the cashews in a bowl and add enough cold water to cover them. Cover and let soak overnight in the refrigerator. Drain and rinse the cashews, then put them in a blender. Add the coconut meat, coconut oil, agave nectar, and vanilla bean and process for 2 minutes, until very smooth. Transfer to a bowl, cover, and chill in the refrigerator for 1 hour.

To make the granola, soak the dates and raisins in hot water until softened, about 2 hours.

Preheat the oven to 150°F. Line 2 rimmed baking sheets with parchment paper.

Drain the fruit, transfer to a food processor fitted with the metal blade, and process until coarsely ground. Add the maple syrup, vanilla, salt, orange zest, and orange juice and pulse to combine. Transfer to a large bowl.

Put the cashews, sunflower seeds, almonds, and pecans in the food processor and pulse until broken up. Add to the date mixture, along with the pumpkin seeds and coconut, and stir or toss with your hands until well coated. Spread the granola mixture on the baking sheets and bake until crisp, about 2 hours.

Meanwhile, to make the topping, put the peaches, agave nectar, orange juice, and vanilla bean in a bowl and toss together. Spread the mixture out on a rimmed baking sheet and bake, along with the granola, until juicy, about 30 minutes. Let cool, then transfer to a bowl. Cover and refrigerate.

Remove the vanilla bean from the topping. Spoon the granola into the bottom of a parfait or martini glass. Top with a spoonful of the cashew cream, and then the topping.

Doughnuts

Whether you dunk these delicious, light and airy doughnuts in your morning coffee or nibble on them after dinner for dessert, they are irresistible. We serve them with powdery confectioners' sugar, cinnamon sugar, or chocolate sauce. We like to fry these doughnuts in sunflower oil because it has no flavor and a high smoking point, which is beneficial for quick frying. Note that the dough must rise overnight before using.

1½ cups warm water (about 110°F)
2 tablespoons active dry yeast
½ cup unrefined sugar
2½ cups unbleached all-purpose flour
¼ cup Ener-G egg replacer
1 teaspoon sea salt
¼ cup safflower oil
Sunflower or safflower oil, for frying
Confectioners' sugar, cinnamon sugar, or chocolate sauce, for serving
Chocolate Sauce (see page 145)

Makes about 12 doughnuts

Put the water in a bowl. Add the yeast and ¼ cup of the sugar, stir, and let sit for 15 minutes.

In a large bowl, mix the flour, egg replacer, salt, and remaining ¼ cup of sugar together. Add the safflower oil and mix again. Add the yeast mixture and mix with floured hands until the dough is smooth and not sticky, adding more flour if needed. Shape into a ball, place in a bowl, cover with plastic wrap, and leave in a warm place to rise overnight.

When ready to cook the doughnuts, roll the dough out ½ inch thick. Using a 3-inch ring mold or biscuit cutter, cut out dough rounds. Gather the scraps, roll them out again, and cut out more dough rounds until all the dough is used.

Heat 3 inches of sunflower oil in a deep cast-iron skillet over medium-high heat. Fry the doughnuts in batches until golden brown, about 2 minutes per side. Transfer to paper towels to drain and cool.

Sprinkle the doughnuts with confectioners' sugar or cinnamon sugar or drizzle with chocolate sauce and serve.

Chocolate Mousse Tower

The Chocolate Mousse Tower is Candle 79's signature dessert, and it's a decadent treat. It can be paired with almond or peanut butter mousse and garnished with peanuts, almonds, or cashews. At the restaurant we usually form the towers using ring molds, but ramekins work just as well. Note that the mousse must set overnight in the refrigerator before unmolding and serving.

2½ cups vegan semisweet chocolate chips
1 cup soy milk
1 pound silken tofu
¾ cup maple syrup
Chocolate shavings, for garnish
Peanuts, almonds, or cashews, for garnish (optional)

Serves 6

Put the chocolate chips and soy milk in the top of a double boiler set over simmering water. Cook, stirring occasionally, until the chocolate has melted. Set aside to cool a bit.

Put the tofu, maple syrup, and melted chocolate mixture in a blender and process until smooth, about 3 minutes. Lightly coat six 3 by 1-inch ring molds or ramekins with safflower oil. Divide the chocolate mixture equally between the molds and chill in the refrigerator overnight.

Unmold each tower, garnish with chocolate shavings and nuts, if desired, and serve at once. If using ramekins, serve directly from the ramekins.

Drinks

At Candle 79, our organic wine and cocktail bar is quite a scene! A seat at the bar is the perfect perch to observe the cocktail-mixing secrets of our bar staff, famous for their creative cocktails and fresh, reviving tonics. Recently, we've added organic and sustainably crafted spirits to our bar offerings, and our guests are happily imbibing classics like aromatic gin martinis and seasonal specialties like fresh strawberry margaritas with balsamic sea salt. Here in our book, we've included some of our signature sake and wine cocktails, for which we are best known, along with sippers and tonics for any time of day. We hope you'll use these recipes to inspire your inner mixologist and formulate drinks, with or without spirits, that incorporate seasonal ingredients to create luscious organic libations that will make your party or gathering an event to be remembered.

Apricot Spritzer

We love the sunny, sweet flavor of apricots. This refreshing sipper contains aloe juice, a hydrating and cleansing tonic. We highly recommend George's brand aloe juice, which can be found online or in most natural food stores. This recipe can be adapted to use your favorite seasonal fruit. Our customers also love this one with passion fruit. To make agave simple syrup, stir together equal amounts of agave nectar and water until well blended.

We like to add hydrated chia seeds to many of our drinks because they are a powerful superfood. These healthful edible seeds are high in omega-3 fatty acids and protein, packed with antioxidants, and loaded with vitamins, minerals, and potassium. They are a member of the sage family and are available at natural food stores and online. You can use the variation at the bottom of this recipe to add chia seeds to this spritzer or any of the other drinks in this chapter.

2 ounces apricot purée
1 ounce aloe juice
1 ounce agave simple syrup (see headnote)
$1/2$ ounce freshly squeezed lemon juice
Ice
Sparkling water
Lemon slice, for garnish

Serves 1

Pour the apricot purée, aloe juice, simple syrup, and lemon juice into a 16-ounce glass, then fill with ice. Top off with sparkling water and mix well by transferring the contents to another container and then back into the glass. Garnish with the lemon slice and serve.

Variation: Apricot Spritzer with Chia Seeds

$1^2/3$ ounces water
1 teaspoon chia seeds

To hydrate the seeds, pour the water into a small bowl, then add the chia seeds slowly, stirring constantly so they don't clump. Let stand for 5 minutes, then stir the seeds once more. Let sit for another 10 minutes or until the seeds are competely hydrated into a gel.

Stir 1 or 2 teaspoons of the hydrated gel into the prepared drink. The hydrated seeds will keep, covered, in the refrigerator for up to 1 week.

Elderberry Elixir

Elderberry extract is derived from the black elderberry plant. It has long been used as a remedy for the common cold, flu, and respiratory infections and is believed to be a powerful immune and circulatory system booster. We add it to fresh apple and lemon juices for a delightful, restorative drink. Elderberry extract is available at natural food stores, organic grocers, and online.

½ ounce elderberry extract
½ ounce freshly squeezed lemon
    juice
7 ounces apple juice, preferably
    freshly pressed
Lemon slice, for garnish

Serves 1

Pour the elderberry extract and lemon juice into an 8-ounce glass. Add the apple juice and stir. Garnish with the lemon slice and serve.

Ginger Ale

One of our most popular beverages here at Candle 79—our wonderful fresh ginger ale—is a thirst-quenching, spicy, pick-me-up for any time of day. And it's healthy to boot! In studies, ginger has been shown to aid digestion, alleviate nausea, and improve circulation. Ginger juice can be extracted from fresh ginger with a juicer or garlic press or purchased from a natural foods store. To make agave simple syrup, stir together equal parts of agave nectar and water until completely mixed. Note: you can make a more traditional simple syrup by heating equal parts unrefined cane sugar and water on the stove until the sugar dissolves completely. Or substitute a different sweetener of your choice.

½ ounce ginger juice or 1 tablespoon
    grated ginger
1 ounce freshly squeezed lemon juice
1½ ounces agave simple syrup
    (see headnote)
Ice
Sparkling water
Mint sprig, for garnish
Lemon slice, for garnish

Serves 1

Pour the ginger juice, lemon juice, and simple syrup into a 16-ounce glass, then fill with ice. Top off with sparkling water and mix well by transferring contents to another container and then back into the glass. Garnish with the mint sprig and lemon slice and serve.

Coconut-Mint Frappé

This reviving frappé is made with fresh avocado and coconut water. Coconut water is a nutritional wonder. It is low in natural sugars, full of vitamins, and contains more potassium and less sodium than most energy drinks. Coconut water is available fresh or packaged at juice bars, natural food stores such as Whole Foods, and online.

½ ripe avocado, pitted, peeled, and chopped
8 ounces young coconut water, preferably fresh (see headnote)
1 ounce agave nectar
1½ teaspoons freshly squeezed lime juice
10 fresh mint leaves, plus 1 mint sprig for garnish (optional)
1 cup ice

Serves 1

Put the avocado, coconut water, agave nectar, lime juice, mint leaves, and ice in a blender and process on high speed until smooth. Pour the mixture into a 16-ounce glass, garnish with the sprig of mint if desired, and serve.

Summer Sangria

Dry rosé wine is the thing to drink on hot summer evenings, and cold sangria made with fresh ripe fruit and rosé is perfection. A finishing splash of Prosecco or sparkling rosé adds a very festive touch to this beautiful, refreshing drink. Note that some of the fruit must soak in the rosé overnight.

1 (750 ml) bottle of dry rosé
1 firm peach, halved, pitted, and
    diced
1 orange, thinly sliced and quartered
¼ cup freshly squeezed lemon juice
¼ cup unrefined sugar
2 ounces Cointreau or any orange
    liqueur, such as Citry (see
    Resources, page 182)
2 ounces brandy
1 cup fresh strawberries, stemmed
    and sliced
½ cup fresh blueberries
Prosecco, sparkling rosé,
    or sparkling water

Serves 6

Combine the rosé, peach, orange, lemon juice, sugar, Cointreau, and brandy in a large pitcher. Stir until the sugar dissolves. Refrigerate overnight.

Before serving, add the strawberries and blueberries. Pour over ice into sturdy wine goblets, add a splash of Prosecco, and serve.

Winter Spiced Sangria

Although we usually think of sangria as a summery drink, this version made with spicy Zinfandel, fruit, and spices is a good thing to sip in the winter in front of a roaring fire. We also use this recipe to make a hot mulled wine that's the perfect libation for Christmas Eve or any holiday party. Simply combine the ingredients in a saucepan, heat over medium heat until it reaches a simmer, let simmer for 3 minutes, stirring occasionally, and then serve immediately with the recommended garnishes.

1 (750 ml) bottle of Zinfandel
4 ounces pear nectar
2 ounces Cointreau
2 ounces crème de cassis
¼ cup unrefined sugar
4 whole cloves
2 whole star anise pods
3 cinnamon sticks, plus 6 cinnamon
   sticks for garnish
3 oranges, thinly sliced into rounds,
   6 slices reserved for garnish
1 pear, peeled, cored, and cut into
   small pieces
1 apple, peeled, cored, and cut into
   small pieces

Serves 6

Combine the wine, pear nectar, Cointreau, crème de cassis, sugar, cloves, star anise, 3 cinnamon sticks, oranges (reserving 6 slices for garnish), pear, and apple in a large pitcher and stir until the sugar dissolves. Refrigerate overnight.

Serve over ice in sturdy wine goblets, garnishing each glass with a cinnamon stick and a slice of orange.

Cherry Pie

This organic, all-American cocktail tastes just like a slice of Grandma's cherry pie with graham cracker crust! To make agave simple syrup, stir together equal amounts of agave nectar and water until well blended. If you can't obtain the French vanilla syrup, substitute a drop of pure vanilla extract and ½ ounce more agave simple syrup.

2 tablespoons crushed vegan graham
    crackers
½ teaspoon unrefined sugar
Pinch of ground cinnamon
Lemon wedge
4 ounces organic sake
½ ounce freshly squeezed lemon
    juice
1 ounce cherry juice
½ ounce agave simple syrup
    (see headnote)
½ teaspoon French vanilla syrup
    (see Resources, page 182)
Ice

Serves 1

Put the graham cracker crumbs, sugar, and cinnamon onto a small plate and mix with your fingers. Moisten the rim of a martini glass with the lemon wedge. Turn the glass upside down into the plate of crumbs to coat.

Combine the sake, lemon juice, cherry juice, simple syrup, and vanilla syrup in a cocktail shaker half filled with ice. Shake vigorously. Strain into the rimmed glass and serve.

Pomegranate Cosmo

This twist on the classic Cosmo is Candle 79's ode to the eighties! Pomegranate is a powerful antioxidant that balances this sweet and tart cocktail. We like to use Sho Chiku Bai Nama Sake, made from organic rice harvested from California's Sacramento Valley, with no preservatives, no brewer's alcohol added, and no sulfites. It has a full, fresh, fruity but dry flavor perfect for sake cocktails like this one. To make agave simple syrup, stir together equal amounts of agave nectar and water until well blended.

4 ounces organic sake
1 ounce pomegranate juice
½ ounce freshly squeezed lime juice
1 ounce agave simple syrup (see headnote)
½ ounce Cointreau or any orange liqueur, such as Citry (see Resources, page 182)
Ice
Lime slice, for garnish
Fresh pomegranate seeds, for garnish

Serves 1

Combine the sake, pomegranate juice, lime juice, simple syrup, and Cointreau in a cocktail shaker half filled with ice. Shake, then strain into a martini glass, garnish with the lime slice and pomegranate seeds, and serve.

Mango Margarita

Sweet and juicy Mango Margaritas are a fun and festive complement to our Mexican-inspired dishes.

2 lime slices, one reserved for
    garnish
Sea salt
4 ounces organic sake
2 ounces mango puree or nectar, or
    3 ounces muddled fresh mango
½ ounce Cointreau or any orange
    liqueur, such as Citry (see
    Resources, page 182)
1 ounce freshly squeezed lime juice
Ice

Serves 1

Wet the rim of a margarita or martini glass with one of the lime slices. Turn the glass upside down into a shallow plate of salt to coat the rim.

Combine the sake, mango puree, Cointreau, and lime juice in a cocktail shaker half filled with ice. Shake vigorously. Strain into the rimmed glass, garnish with the remaining lime slice, and serve.

French 79

The French 79 is an elegant champagne cocktail and our rendition of the classic French 75. We named it after our location on East 79th street, and it quickly became our signature cocktail. Enjoy the bubbly burst of flavor from this colorful, delicious drink. It's perfect for showers, festive brunches, and cocktail parties. To make agave simple syrup, stir together equal amounts of agave nectar and water until well blended.

2 ounces organic sake
1 ounce mango or papaya puree
½ ounce freshly squeezed lemon juice
¾ ounce agave simple syrup (see headnote)
¼ ounce crème de cassis
2 ounces sparkling wine
¼ ounce pomegranate juice
Blackberry, for garnish (optional)

Serves 1

Combine the sake, mango puree, lemon juice, and simple syrup in a cocktail shaker half filled with ice. Shake and strain into a champagne flute. Tilt the glass and slowly slide in the crème de cassis so it sinks to the bottom of the glass. Top with the sparkling wine.

Slowly pour the pomegranate juice into the glass while vigorously whisking the upper one-third of the liquid with a straw to create a layering effect. The crème de cassis should sit on the bottom, with the pomegranate juice and champagne creating the top layer and the sake-mango mixture forming the middle layer. Garnish the rim with a blackberry, if desired, then serve.

The Grapevine

Chock full of antioxidants, Concord grapes are a flavorful powerhouse from the vineyard. This juicy cocktail will bring back memories of childhood in a deliciously healthy and sophisticated way! Organic Concord grape juice concentrate can be found online at websites like NaturesFlavors.com and at natural food stores. To make agave simple syrup, stir together equal amounts of agave nectar and water until well blended.

4 ounces organic sake
1 ounce Concord grape juice
½ ounce freshly squeezed lime juice
½ ounce agave simple syrup (see headnote)
6 fresh mint leaves
Ice
Sparkling water

Serves 1

Combine the sake, grape juice, lime juice, simple syrup, and mint leaves in a cocktail shaker half filled with ice. Shake well, then pour the contents, including the ice and mint, into a rocks glass or strain into an 8-ounce martini glass. Top with a splash of sparkling water and serve.

Ginger Rush

A spicy, warming all-time favorite of our guests, the Ginger Rush has been on our cocktail menu since we opened our doors in 2003. It's like having a ginger and plum tart in a glass! You can either juice the ginger yourself by running large chunks of ginger through your juicer, or buy bottled ginger juice online at sites like GingerPeople.com or at specialty and natural food stores like Whole Foods. To make agave simple syrup, stir together equal amounts of agave nectar and water until well blended.

4 ounces organic sake
1 ounce plum nectar
¾ ounce fresh ginger juice
  (see headnote)
¾ ounce agave simple syrup
  (see headnote)
½ ounce freshly squeezed lemon
  juice
Ice
1 stick of peeled fresh ginger,
  for garnish

Serves 1

Put the sake, plum nectar, ginger juice, simple syrup, and lemon juice in a cocktail shaker half filled with ice and shake vigorously. Strain into a martini glass, garnish with the ginger stick, and serve.

Sake Mojito Classico

Traditional mojitos are made with rum and muddled mint. Our version is made with organic sake and fresh mint from a local organic farm. This is a very light and refreshing drink.

7 fresh mint leaves, plus 1 mint sprig
   for garnish
1½ teaspoons unrefined sugar
½ lime, cut into half wheels, 1 half
   wheel reserved for garnish
4 ounces organic sake
Ice
1 ounce sparkling water

Serves 1

Muddle the mint leaves with the sugar and lime (reserving 1 half wheel for garnish) in a cocktail shaker. Add the sake, fill the shaker halfway with ice, and shake well. Pour the entire mixture into a highball glass. Top with the sparkling water, garnish with the mint sprig and reserved lime, and serve.

Mixed Berry Sake Mojito

This mojito is made with organic sake, a combination of beautiful fresh berries and mint, and a squeeze of lime. This refreshing cocktail is as pretty to look at as it is delicious to drink, and we love to make a batch to serve on a summer evening.

7 fresh mint leaves, plus 1 mint sprig
   for garnish
1 teaspoon unrefined sugar
½ lime, cut into half wheels, 1 half
   wheel reserved for garnish
1 small handful of mixed fresh
   berries, such as 2 large
   strawberries, 6 blueberries,
   and 4 raspberries
4 ounces organic sake
Ice
1 ounce sparkling water

Serves 1

Muddle the mint leaves with the sugar, lime (reserving 1 half wheel for garnish), and berries in a cocktail shaker. Add the sake, fill the shaker halfway with ice, and shake well. Pour the entire mixture into a highball glass. Top with the sparkling water, garnish with the mint sprig and reserved lime, and serve.

Cucumber-Basil Martini

The flavors of fresh cucumber and basil blend together beautifully in this summery quaff. This is an especially cooling drink, the kind you dream of after a dip in the pool. Note: To juice cucumbers, quarter them lengthwise and run them through a juicer. One pound of cucumbers will make about 1 cup of juice, enough for 4 cocktails. Leaving the skins on will make a darker colored juice and will increase the nutritional content, especially the amount of vitamin A. Leftover juice is an excellent cooling beverage. If you do not have access to a juicer, simply muddle two ½-inch slices of whole cucumber with the basil per drink. To make agave simple syrup, stir together equal amounts of agave nectar and water until well blended.

4 ounces organic sake
2 ounces fresh cucumber juice (see headnote)
½ ounce freshly squeezed lemon juice
½ ounce agave simple syrup (see headnote)
3 fresh basil leaves, torn
Ice
Lemon twist, for garnish

Serves 1

Combine the sake, cucumber juice, lemon juice, simple syrup, and basil in a cocktail shaker half filled with ice. Shake well and strain into a chilled 8-ounce martini glass. Garnish with the lemon twist and serve.

ORGANIC BEERS

As a fresh, flavorful alternative to wine and cocktails, beer pairs beautifully with vegan cuisine. One of our favorite organic breweries is Wolaver's in Vermont. One of the first certified organic breweries in the nation, Wolaver's has been a leader in sustainable brewing since 1997. Wolaver's philosophy in producing their beers is much in line with our own: to create a local, organic, collective, green, and handcrafted product. Try their crisp, mellow, rich Brown Ale with our Black Bean–Chipotle Burgers (page 95) and Polenta Fries (page 104). For fall, they make a delightful Pumpkin Ale, perfect with hearty tempeh dishes garnished with fruit chutneys, or a chocolaty Mexican mole sauce (page 83).

For summer salads with fruity accents, we love Schneider Edel-Weisse, an organic hefeweizen that is beautifully crisp and citrusy with hints of spice. This is an elegant brew—serve it in a wine goblet with our Seitan Piccata (page 89) for a fresh, modern approach to pairing.

GLOSSARY

AGAVE NECTAR This natural sweetener derived from a succulent cactuslike plant has the color and consistency of honey. A very versatile syrup used in many desserts and drinks, agave nectar has much less impact on blood sugar (with a lower glycemic index and glycemic load) than cane sugar does.

ANCHO CHILE A dried poblano chile pepper, it is the sweetest of the dried chiles, with a slightly fruity flavor that ranges from mild to pungent.

ARAME A sea vegetable, arame is rich in calcium, potassium, iron, protein, and vitamins A, B1, and B2. Use in salads and with vegetables and tofu.

ARROWROOT POWDER A thickening agent made from arrowroot, a tropical tuber, this powder is gluten free, more easily digested than wheat flour, and high in calcium. Use in puddings, sauces, and other foods.

BLACK GARLIC Rich in antioxidants, this is garlic fermented at high heat, which turns the cloves black. The taste is sweet and syrupy, with hints of balsamic vinegar and tamarind.

BROWN RICE VINEGAR Made from brown rice wine, this vinegar is organic, naturally brown, unfiltered, and unpasteurized.

CHIPOTLE CHILE Dried, smoked jalapeño peppers, called chipotles, are available in whole or ground form. They are very hot and spicy. Use to season soups, sauces, and sandwich spreads.

COCONUT MILK Made by adding water to shredded coconut meat and squeezing out the essence of the coconut meat, coconut milk is a great alternative to animal-based dairy products in sauces and desserts.

EGG REPLACER Ener-G Foods makes the most popular and widely available type of egg replacer, and that's what our recipes call for. This dairy-free, gluten-free powder blends potato starch and tapioca flour with other ingredients to create a dairy-free and gluten-free substitute for eggs in baking. It is versatile, easy to use, and available at most natural food stores, some larger well-stocked grocery stores, and online.

ELDERBERRY When cooked, the small dark berries from elderberry bushes add a sweet, tangy flavor to elixirs, syrups, jams, pie fillings, and more. Elderberries contain potassium and large amounts of vitamin C and are thought to boost the immune system.

EPAZOTE A pungent herb with a flavor similar to coriander, epazote is commonly used in Mexican and Southwestern cooking and is most often sold in dried form. It is often added to beans as it helps to reduce gas.

FLAXSEEDS Both flaxseeds and their oil are rich in omega-3 fatty acids. Flaxseed oil is very nutritious and easy to digest, and is great in salad dressings and sauces, on cereals and porridge, over popcorn, and as a spread for breads. The oil should never be heated. The seeds can add flavor and texture to breakfast cereal, granola, crackers, and breads.

GINGER JUICE Ginger has been shown to aid digestion, alleviate nausea, and improve circulation. Ginger juice can be extracted from fresh ginger with a juicer or garlic press, or purchased from a natural foods store.

GLUTEN-FREE FOOD Foods that are free of wheat, rye, barley, oats, spelt, triticale, and any derivatives of these grains.

GUAJILLO CHILE A mild dried chile popular in Mexican cooking, the guajillo (little gourd, in Spanish) is deep red in color, with a green tea and berry flavor.

HEMP SEEDS Edible and easily digested, with a nutty flavor, hemp seeds contain all the essential amino acids and fatty acids necessary for good health. They are also rich in protein and omega-3 fatty acids. We think this condiment should be on every table.

HIJIKI A sea vegetable that is very high in calcium, phosphorus, iron, protein, and vitamins A, B1, and B2. Use in soups and salads and as a garnish.

KOMBU Japanese cooks use this sea vegetable to boost flavor and also add texture. Kombu is very high in calcium, phosphorus, iron, protein, and vitamins A, B1, B2, and C. Chop soaked kombu and add to salads and vegetables. Add unsoaked kombu (or reserved soaking liquid) to soups for a rich stock.

LIVE FOODS Plant-based foods that still contain their natural enzymes are referred to as live, raw, or living foods. Cooking food above 118°F kills all natural enzymes and changes the food's molecular content, which can sometimes render it toxic. Live foods contain a vast array of vital nutrients that are essential to maintaining a healthy body.

MISO Fermented soybean paste that is influenced by its aging process, which can range from six months to three years, is called miso. There are three categories of miso: barley miso, which is dark in color; soybean miso, which is medium in color; and rice miso, the lightest in color. This mainstay of Japanese cooking is rich in amino acids and live enzymes, and is an excellent source of protein as well as a remarkable digestive aid. Use the lighter (white) miso in delicate soups, broths, and sauces, and darker miso in heavier dishes.

MOLE There are many types of mole, a classic Mexican sauce whose name is derived from the Spanish word for concoction. One of the most familiar outside of Mexico is a rich, dark blend of onions, garlic, ground nuts or seeds, several types of chiles, and chocolate.

MULATO CHILE This popular dried chile is similar in appreareance to an ancho chile, but a bit darker and sweeter, with a mild heat and earthy flavor. Ancho and mulato chiles are interchangeable in a recipe.

NORI A black sea vegetable, nori is very high in calcium, phosphorus, iron, protein, potassium, magnesium, iodine, and vitamins A, B1, B2, C, D, and niacin. Sprinkle torn, chopped, or ground pieces over vegetables, grains, and salads. Make nori rolls with rice and vegetable fillings. Nori is sold as raw or toasted sheets.

NUTRITIONAL YEAST As dried flakes or powder—both forms derived from yeast—nutritional yeast is used in small amounts to add fullness and flavor to soups, stocks, and salad dressings. It's high in vitamins and minerals such as B12, which is often lacking in a vegan diet.

OLIVE OIL Olive oil has many health benefits, including lowering LDL cholesterol levels, blood sugar levels, and blood pressure. It also contains antioxidants such as vitamin E and cartenoids. In most of our cooking, we use extra-virgin olive oil, but you can also use a less expensive blend of extra-virgin and regular olive oils or a commercial-grade olive oil. The smoke point of olive oil varies with its quality. Extra-virgin olive oil has a high smoke point and lesser quality olive oils have a much lower smoke point.

PANKO These Japanese bread crumbs have a lighter, crispier, and flakier texture than their Western counterparts. They are great for breading as they tend to stay crispy longer and absorb seasoning well.

PASILLA CHILE A dried version of the chilaca chile, the pasilla is dark and wrinkled, with a mild, sweet flavor. Mexican mole sauces typically include it as a standard ingredient.

QUINOA A grain first cultivated by the Incas, quinoa is a complete protein packed with lysine and other amino acids. It's also a rich source of calcium, iron, phosphorus, various B vitamins, and vitamin E. It adds a hearty, nutty flavor to salads, soups, and hot cereals.

RAMPS Wild onions that resemble a green onion with broad leaves, ramps have a garlicky onion flavor that will add an interesting twist to a dish. One of the first green vegetables to sprout in spring, ramps are only available from March through June.

SAKE A rice-based alcoholic beverage, we recommend Sho Chiku Bai Nama Sake, which is made from organice rice with no preservatives, added brewer's alcohol, or sulfites. Its full, fresh, fruity but dry flavor is perfect for sake cocktails.

SEA SALT This type of salt is derived from evaporated seawater and is high in trace minerals. It comes in fine-grained and larger crystals.

SEITAN To make seitan, whole wheat bread flour is rinsed with water to extract the gluten, producing a food that is naturally high in protein and low in carbohydrates and fat. Dubbed "wheat meat" and considered the ultimate meat substitute, seitan is often served as a main course in vegan cooking.

SOY MILK When soybeans are soaked in water, ground, rehydrated, then filtered, you get soy milk. This beverage is a good source of vegetable protein. Packaged organic brands are readily available.

TAHINI Rich in calcium, phosphorus, and protein, tahini is hulled sesame seeds ground into a paste and a staple of the Middle Eastern diet.

TAMARI This is a traditional, naturally made soy sauce, as distinguished from chemically processed soy sauce. Tamari also contains a higher ratio of soybeans and is available wheat free (our preference).

TAMARIND Popular in Indian and Middle Eastern cuisine, tamarind is a small datelike fruit. It is available in many forms: concentrated pulp, dried pods, powder, paste, and syrup. Tamarind has the flavor of sour prunes and is often used to season chutneys, soups, curries, and bean dishes.

TAPIOCA-BASED CHEESE The starch extracted from the root of the cassava plant is the base for this dairy-free cheese. It's allergen free and melts better than other nondairy alternatives. We recommend the Daiya brand.

TEMPEH This traditional Indonesian fermented soy product is heartier than tofu, with a chewy texture and nutty flavor. Tempeh is high in protein and easily digestible. Flattened, sweetened strips of tempeh are used like bacon in vegan sandwiches and with breakfast and brunch dishes.

TOFU Formed of soy milk curds, tofu is a source of high-quality protein and is rich in calcium and cholesterol free. Tofu comes in a variety of consistencies, from silken to extra firm. Different dishes require different levels of firmness.

UMEBOSHI VINEGAR The brine from making umeboshi (Japanese pickled plums) has a fruity, sour flavor and many of the nutritional benefits of umeboshi. The alkalizing effect it has on the body reduces fatigue, eliminates toxins, and stimulates digestion. Though technically not a vinegar because it contains salt, it is a great substitute for vinegar in salad dressings or when cooking your favorite vegetables.

VEGAN BUTTERY SPREAD This dairy-free margarine is made from soybeans and has a buttery texture. Use in baking and sauces and as a spread. We recommend the Earth Balance brand.

WAKAME An edible sea vegetable that is popular in Asian cuisine, wakame has a slightly sweet flavor that makes it a great addition to soups and salads.

UNREFINED SUGAR Made from the juice of the sugarcane plant, unrefined sugar retains some of the minerals and nutrients lost in the refining process of conventional sugars. Additionally, unrefined sugars don't require some of the harmful chemicals that are used in the refining process.

VEGAN MAYONNAISE A cholesterol- and animal product–free version of mayonnaise, vegan mayonnaise is made by replacing the eggs with soy, nuts, or various oils. It is available prepared in natural food stores or is easy to make at home and can be substituted for conventional mayonnaise in any recipe. There is a great recipe for homemade vegan mayo in *The Candle Cafe Cookbook*.

YUCA The root vegetable yuca is a starchy vegetable similar to a potato. Also known as cassava, yuca is a great source of carbohydrates and contains vitamins A, B, and C.

RESOURCES

Bionaturae
860-642-6996
www.bionaturae.com
Organic fruit nectars

Coombs Family Farms
888-266-6271
www.coombsfamilyfarms.com
American organic maple syrup

Daiya Foods, Inc.
604-569-0530
www.daiyafoods.com
Allergen-free tapioca-based cheese

Earth Balance
201-421-3970
www.earthbalancenatural.com
Dairy-free buttery spreads

Earthbound Farms
800-690-3200
www.ebfarm.com
Non-GMO and organic salads, fruits, and
vegetables

Eden Foods, Inc.
888-424-3336
www.edenfoods.com
Specialty organic products

Edward & Sons
805-684-8500
www.edwardandsons.com
Organic and vegan specialties, coconut milk, and
coconut cream

Ener-G Foods Inc.
800-331-5222
www.ener-g.com
Gluten-free specialty foods and egg replacer

Excalibur Dehydrators
800-875-4254
www.excaliburdehydrator.com
Dehydrators

Exotic Superfoods
917-685-2586
www.exoticsuperfoods.com
Organic and raw coconut meat and water

Field Roast Grain Meat Co.
800-311-9497
www.fieldroast.com
Artisan and vegan grain-based meats and sausages

Fillo Factory
800-653-4556
www.fillofactory.com
All types of phyllo (fillo) products

Flavorganics
973-344-8014, extension 109
www.flavorganics.com
Organic syrups and flavor extracts

Follow Your Heart
818-725-2820
www.followyourheart.com
Veganaise and vegan cheeses

Four Seasons Produce, Inc.
800-422-8384
www.fsproduce.com
Organic produce

Fresh Tofu Inc.
610-433-4711
www.freshtofu.com
Certified organic tofu, tempeh, and seitan

Frontier Natural Products
800-669-3275
www.frontiercoop.com
Herbs and spices

Goldmine Natural Food Company
800-475-3663
www.goldminenaturalfood.com
Organic and heirloom foods

Greenbar Collective
626-771-9469
www.greenbar.biz
Organic and eco-friendly liquors such as Tru
Vodka and Citry Orange Liqueur

Los Chileros de Nuevo Mexico
888-328-2445
www.loschileros.com
Organic dried chiles and pure chile powders

Lundberg Family Farms
530-882-4551
www.lundberg.com
Rice and rice-based products

Maine Coast Sea Vegetables
207-565-2907
www.seaveg.com
Sea vegetables

Navitas Naturals
888-645-4282
www.navitasnaturals.com
Organic cashews, cacao, wakame, nori, fruits
and berries

Puro Verde Spirits
979-690-3321
www.puroverdespirits.com
Organic tequilas

Quinoa Corporation
310-217-8125
www.quinoa.net
Ancient Harvest quinoa products: organic, non-
GMO, and gluten-free quinoa, quinoa flour, and
quinoa-corn pastas

Rapunzel Pure Organics
973-338-1499
www.rapunzel.com
Organic yeasts, chocolate, and sugar products

Satur Farms
631-734-4219
www.saturfarms.com
Specialty salads greens, leafy vegetables, heirloom tomatoes, root vegetables, and herbs, grown
on Long Island and available online

Shady Maple Farm Ltd.
819-362-3241
www.shadymaple.ca
Canadian organic maple syrup, sugar, and
cookies

South River Miso
413-369-4057
www.southrivermiso.com
Organic miso products

Spectrum Naturals, Inc.
800-434-4246
www.spectrumorganics.com
All-natural, organic, and artisan oils and spreads

Sunspire Natural Chocolates
866-972-6879
www.sunspire.com
All natural, organic, fair-trade, and dairy-free
chocolate

truRoots
925-218-2205
www.truroots.com
Organic sprouted and whole grains and beans

Twin Marquis
718-386-6868
www.twinmarquis.com
Asian specialty items, including vegan wonton
wrappers

Vitamix Corp.
800-848-2649
www.vitamix.com
Vitamix blender

Whole Foods
www.wholefoods.com
Largest retailer of natural and organic foods

Wholesome Sweeteners
800-680-1896
www.wholesomesweeteners.com
Organic and all natural sweeteners and
unrefined sugars

ACKNOWLEDGMENTS

We at Candle 79 have many many people to thank, including our restaurant staff in both the front and the back of the house and our millions of beloved customers: *We thank you!* First and foremost, we thank our founding father, the person who is responsible for holding the whole enchilada together: Bart Potenza. His lottery win started this business over sixteen years ago, and his wit, integrity, and ongoing love for both Candle restaurants have kept them burning brightly. He pays it forward while paying the bills, and he always makes it look easy.

Candle 79 would not be what it is today without the loving kindness, professionalism, and leadership of Benay Vynerib, whose extraordinary commitment keeps us on point every day. Special thanks go to Francesca MacAaron for generously sharing her deep knowledge of wine. Her close working relationships with vintners from all over the world made the wine pairings and drinks chapter in the book very special. Francesca and Benay put their hearts into every Candle 79 meal and were instrumental in shaping this project. Thanks also to bar chef Kyle Bullen and the bar team, Josh, Chris, Robert, and Jake, for contributing their master mixologist skills to the drinks chapter of this book.

It takes a proverbial village to run a restaurant. Hats off to our entire staff at Candle 79 and Candle Cafe, as well as the farmers, purveyors, truckers, and delivery people who keep our kitchen well stocked with the finest ingredients imaginable. We have a constant attitude of gratitude to them all.

We thank our good friends Kathy Freston, Tal Ronnen, Chloe Jo Davis, John Joseph, Kris Carr, Dr. T. Colin Campbell, John Mackey, Gene Baur, Robin Quivers, Biz Stone, Margot Schupf, Dr. Mehmet Oz, Tracey and Michael J. Fox, Alicia Silverstone, and Woody, Laura, Deni, Zoe and Makani Harrelson, for their ongoing work and support of our shared passion for extraordinary vegan cuisine and for making the world a friendlier, greener, healthier, and happier place to live.

Thanks and gratitude to the many people who worked so hard on this cookbook:

To Rory Freedman for writing the tremendous foreword that opens this book. The way you expressed your love for Candle 79 warms our hearts, and you continue to inspire us with all that you do.

To those who contributed to recipe development: Daniel Biron, Katelyn Stone, the Desantis family, Mimi Clark, Susan Mason, Laura Felenstein, Rossella Galli, and Annette and Emily Doskow. Thanks for testing, tasting, and writing it all down.

To Rita Maas and her assistants, Elizabeth Drago and Sheri Manson, for the incredible photography in this book. And to prop stylists Lynda White and Jeff Wood, who made our food look as good as it tastes.

To the dedicated and talented team at Ten Speed Press: Aaron Wehner, Lisa Westmoreland, Nancy Austin, Katy Brown,

Kara Van de Water, and numerous others, for their sharp editorial and design skills, and for their insight, support, and patience.

To Mark Doskow for keeping the project on track and moving forward from beginning to end. His commitment, creativity, sense of organization, and grace under fire were inspiring.

To our editorial and design consultant, Barbara Scott-Goodman, for helping develop the beautiful look of the book, for pulling the creative team together, and for writing our recipes accurately and into an easy-to-follow style for the home cook.

To Eric Adjei, our CFO, who has been part of our Candle history for twenty-six years. You are a blessing. Thanks for writing the checks, Eric!

To our supportive, loving, and growing families: Vaj, Shelby, Dylan, and Leia; Rosemary, Jeremiah, and Junius; Flora and Jesus; and Brad, Grant, Laura, and Tammy.

And finally, to the Candle 79 cooks and chefs, especially Augustin Tapia, whose creative and innovative cuisine is what keeps our customers coming from all over the world to dine with us every day. Thanks for sharing your talent and for all of your hard work. You inspire us to learn, cook, and grow as an environmentally conscious company and to be the best so we can serve the best. Cheers!

ABOUT THE AUTHORS

 **Joy Pierson** has been a nutritional counselor since 1985. She is a graduate of Tufts University and is certified by the Pritikin Longevity Center and the Hippocrates Health Institute. She and her partner, Bart Potenza, established the Candle Cafe and Candle 79 restaurants in 1994 and 2003, respectively. They have also developed a growing catering and wholesale business and are the authors of *The Candle Cafe Cookbook*. Joy has written, lectured, and consulted extensively about food and nutrition and leads workshops and courses on plant-based cooking, diet, and nutrition. She serves as board chair of the New York Coalition for Healthy School Food and is also an active member of Social Venture Network. She has appeared on the Food Network, the *Today Show*, *Good Morning America*, and *Good Day New York*, among others. Her quest and vision is to continue changing people's awareness of health and well-being and their effect on the planet and future generations by bringing farm-fresh, plant-based food to as many people and as many tables as possible.

 Executive chef **Angel Ramos** began cooking at Candle Cafe. He brought his innovative cooking talents to Candle 79 when it opened and has continued to take vegan cooking to new creative heights with a flair for combining the right mix of flavors and ingredients with multicultural influences. He has also worked as a consultant for events held at the Plaza Hotel, Cipriani Wall Street, and the Beverly Hills Hotel. His recipes have been featured in the *New York Times*, where he was acknowledged for his mastery of vegan organic cuisine, *Vegetarian Times*, and *Pilates Style* magazine. In 2010, Angel was named the *VegNews* Chef of the Year and received an honorable mention from "People's Platelist," on ABC's *Nightline*, in which viewers selected their favorite chefs. He has twice been honored to have his food featured at events at the James Beard House. Angel has helped develop Candle Cafe Frozen Entrées, which are available nationwide. Angel is delighted to share his love of local organic produce in the delicious seasonal menus that he creates for the restaurant.

 Pastry chef and chef de cuisine **Jorge Pineda** has created desserts that have revolutionized vegan baking. In addition to his pastries and famous housemade ice creams that are served at Candle 79, he is still delighting his loyal Candle Cafe customers with his cookies, cakes, pies, and other delicious "hard to believe they're vegan" comfort foods. He was a major contributor to *The Candle Cafe Cookbook*. Jorge's pastries have been featured in the *Los Angeles Times* for the "Best Vegan Desserts in America." Jorge has helped develop Candle Cafe Desserts and Candle Cafe Frozen Entrées, which are available nationwide. He has also consulted and taught plant-based cooking, including work with the New York Coalition for Healthy School Food, Lottie's Kitchen, Macy's, the Waldorf-Astoria, Tavern on the Green, and Cipriani Wall Street.

INDEX

A

Agave nectar, 179
Almond Crumble, 142
Almond Topping, 142
Ancho chile, 179
Appetizers
    Arancini with Roasted Plum
        Tomato Sauce, 15
    Avocado Salsa, 11
    Cashew Cheese–Stuffed Yuca
        Cakes, 18
    Ginger-Seitan Dumplings, 20
    Heirloom Tomato–Avocado
        Tartare, 6
    Roasted Artichokes with Spring
        Vegetables and Crispy Onion
        Rings, 9–10
    Seitan Cakes, 20
    Smoked Paprika Hummus, 17
    Spinach-Mushroom Pâté, 19
    Zucchini Blossom Tempura, 12
Apple-Apricot Strudel, 149
Apricot Chutney, 125
Apricot Spritzer, 158
Arame, 179
Arancini with Roasted Plum Tomato
    Sauce, 15
Arrowroot powder, 179
Artichokes
    Jerusalem Artichoke Soup with
        Crispy Sage Leaves, 33
    Roasted Artichokes with Spring
        Vegetables and Crispy Onion
        Rings, 9–10
Asparagus, Wild Mushroom, and
    Spring Vegetable Crepes, 131
Avocado
    Avocado Salsa, 11
    Chile-Grilled Tofu with Avocado-
        Tomatillo Sauce, 76
    Live Avocado-Cucumber Soup, 26
    Stuffed Avocado with Quinoa
        Pilaf and Chipotle-Avocado
        Dressing, 48

B

Bacon, tempeh, 15
Balsamic-Caramelized Pears, 36
Barbecued Black-Eyed Peas, 100
Basil
    Pan-Seared Pine Nut Pesto
        Tofu, 75
    Pesto, 121
    Pesto Marinade, 75
Beans and legumes
    Barbecued Black-Eyed Peas, 100
    Black Bean and Roasted Poblano
        Soup, 35
    Black Bean–Chipotle Burgers,
        95–96
    Chickpea Crepes, 130
    Moroccan-Spiced Chickpea Cakes,
        66–67
    Smoked Paprika Hummus, 17
    See also Fava beans
Beer, organic, 176
Beet, Fennel, and Fig Salad with
    Cranberry-Sage Dressing, 50
Berries
    Blueberry Butter, 134
    Cranberry-Sage Dressing, 50
    Elderberry Elixir, 159
    Mixed Berry–Sake Mojito, 174
    Raspberry Butter, 138
    Sorbets, 146
    Strawberry Sauce, 142
    Summer Berry Crumble, 142
Black Bean and Roasted Poblano
    Soup, 35
Black Bean–Chipotle Burgers, 95–96
Black-eyed peas, Barbecued, 100
Black garlic, 179

Blood Orange–Fennel Salad, 52
Blueberry Butter, 134
Braised Green Beans, 111
Brown rice vinegar, 179
Butterhead Lettuce, Cauliflower, and
    Red Bell Pepper Salad, 42
Butternut Squash, Mushroom, and
    Sage Crepes, 133
Butternut Squash–Chestnut Soup
    with Caramelized Pears, 36
Butternut Squash Filling, 70

C

Cake, Mexican Chocolate, 144
Candle Cafe Cookbook, 2, 181
Candle 79 restaurant, 1, 2–3
Cashews
    Cashew Cheese, 18, 78
    Cashew Cream, 9
    Cashew Crème Fraîche, 125
    Cashew Parmesan, 63
    Saffron Ravioli with Wild
        Mushrooms and Cashew Cheese,
        69–70
    Vanilla Cashew Cream, 151
Cauliflower, Butterhead Lettuce, and
    Red Bell Pepper Salad, 42
Chard, Sautéed Swiss, 113
Cheese
    Cashew Cheese, 18, 78
    Daiya cheese, 15, 181
    Macadamia Cheese, 40
    Tofu Cheese, 12
    tofu cream cheese, 136
Cherry Pie (drink), 167
Chia seeds, Apricot Spritzer
    with, 158
Chickpea Crepes, 130
Chickpeas Cakes, Moroccan-Spiced,
    66–67

Chile-Grilled Tofu with Avocado-
    Tomatillo Sauce, 76
Chile Sauce, 76
Chipotle-Avocado Dressing, 48
Chipotle chile, 179
Chive Vinaigrette, 46
Chocolate Cake, Mexican, 144
Chocolate Ice Cream, 145
Chocolate Mousse Tower, 154
Chocolate Sauce, 148
Chutney, Apricot, 125
Coconut milk, 179
Coconut-Mint Frappé, 163
Coleslaw, Granny Smith, 101
Corn
    Polenta Fries, 104
    Watercress, Jicama, and Corn
        Salad with Jalapeño Dressing, 43
Cranberry-Sage Dressing, 50
Cream, cashew, 151
Creamed Spinach, 114
Crepes
    Butternut Squash, Mushroom,
        and Sage Crepes, 133
    Chickpea Crepes, 130
    Wild Mushroom, Asparagus, and
        Spring Vegetable Crepes, 131
Cucumbers
    Cucumber-Basil Martini, 176
    Farmers' Market Gazpacho, 29
    Live Avocado-Cucumber Soup, 26
Cutlets, seitan, 109

D
Desserts
    about, 141
    Apple-Apricot Strudel, 149
    Chocolate Ice Cream, 145
    Chocolate Mousse Tower, 154
    Doughnuts, 152
    Mexican Chocolate Cake, 144
    Peach Parfait, 151
    Sorbets, 146
    Summer Berry Crumble, 142
    Vanilla Bean Ice Cream, 144
Daiya cheese, 15, 181

Doughnuts, 152
Dressings
    Chipotle-Avocado Dressing, 48
    Chive Vinaigrette, 46
    Cranberry-Sage Dressing, 50
    Fresh Horseradish Dressing, 45
    Ginger-Sesame Dressing, 49
    Jalapeño Dressing, 43
    Kalamata Olive Vinaigrette, 53
    Pesto Marinade, 75
Drinks
    about, 157
    Apricot Spritzer, 158
    beer, organic, 176
    Cherry Pie, 167
    Coconut-Mint Frappé, 163
    Cucumber-Basil Martini, 176
    Elderberry Elixir, 159
    French 79, 170
    Ginger Ale, 160
    Ginger Rush, 173
    The Grapevine, 172
    Mango Margarita, 169
    Mixed Berry–Sake Mojito, 174
    Pomegranate Cosmo, 168
    Sake Mojito Classico, 174
    Summer Sangria, 165
    wine, 55–56, 57
    Winter Spiced Sangria, 166
Dumplings, Ginger-Seitan, 23

E
Earth Balance Natural Buttery
    Spread, 181
Edamame-Mint Sauce, 124
Egg replacer, 179
Elderberry, 179
Elderberry Elixir, 159
Epazote, 179

F
Farmers' Market Gazpacho, 29
Fava beans
    Wild Mushroom, Asparagus, and
        Spring Vegetable Crepes, 131

Wild Mushroom and Spring
    Vegetable Fricassee, 63
Fennel
    Beet, Fennel, and Fig Salad with
        Cranberry-Sage Dressing, 50
    Blood Orange–Fennel Salad, 52
Flaxseeds, 179
French 79, 170
French Toast, Sourdough, 136
Fries, polenta, 104

G
Gazpacho, Farmers' Market, 29
Ginger
    Ginger Ale, 160
    Gingered Sugar Snap Peas, 112
    Ginger Rush, 173
    Ginger-Seitan Dumplings, 23
    Ginger-Sesame Dressing, 49
    Ginger-Soy Dipping Sauce, 115
    juice, 179
Gluten-free food, 179
Gnocchi, potato, 73–74
Granny Smith Coleslaw, 101
Granola, Nut, 151
The Grapevine, 172
Green beans, Braised, 111
Guajillo chile, 179

H
Heirloom Tomato–Avocado
    Tartare, 6
Heirloom Tomato Salad with
    Macadamia Cheese and Crispy
    Capers, 40
Hemp seeds, 179–80
Herbed Oil Marinade, 64
Herbed Potato-Leek Soup, 34
Herb-Marinated Grilled
    Vegetables, 64
Home-Style Pancakes with
    Blueberry Butter, 134
Horseradish Dressing, Fresh, 45
Huiki, 180
Hummus, Smoked Paprika, 17

I

Ice cream
 Chocolate Ice Cream, 145
 Vanilla Bean Ice Cream, 144

J

Jalapeño Dressing, 43
Jasmine Rice, 106
Jerusalem Artichoke Soup with
 Crispy Sage Leaves, 33
Jicama, Watercress, and Corn Salad
 with Jalapeño Dressing, 43

K

Kale, Vegetable, and Spelt Berry
 Salad with Chive Vinaigrette, 46
Kombu, 180

L

Leeks, Herbed Potato-Leek Soup, 34
Live foods
 about, 180
 Live Avocado-Cucumber Soup, 26
 Live Lasagna, 78

M

Macadamia Cheese and Crispy
 Capers, 40
Mango Margarita, 169
Manicotti Rustica, 71–72
Marinated Tempeh, 108
Mayonnaise, vegan, 181
Mediterranean Salad with Kalamata
 Olive Vinaigrette, 53
Mexican Chocolate Cake, 144
Mint
 Coconut-Mint Frappé, 163
 Edamame-Mint Sauce, 124
 Mint-Cilantro Chimichurri
 Sauce, 120
Miso, 180
Mixed Berry–Sake Mojito, 174
Mixed-Grain Waffles with Raspberry
 Butter, 138
Mole, 180

Moroccan-Spiced Chickpea Cakes,
 66–67
Mulato chile, 180
Mushrooms
 Butternut Squash, Mushroom,
 and Sage Crepes, 133
 Herb-Marinated Grilled
 Vegetables, 64
 Saffron Ravioli with Wild
 Mushrooms and Cashew Cheese,
 69–70
 Sautéed Royal Trumpet
 Mushrooms, 110
 Spinach-Mushroom Pâté, 19
 Wild Mushroom, Asparagus, and
 Spring Vegetable Crepes, 131
 Wild Mushroom and Cipollini
 Salad with Fresh Horseradish
 Dressing, 45
 Wild Mushroom and Spring
 Vegetable Fricassee, 63

N

Nori, 180
Nori- and Sesame-Crusted Seitan, 84
Nut Granola, 151
Nutritional yeast, 180

O

Olive oil, 180
Onion Rings, Crispy, 9
Orange-Fennel Salad, 52

P

Paella, 91–92
Pancakes, Home-Style with
 Blueberry Butter, 134
Panko, 180
Panko-Crusted Seitan Milanese, 86
Pan-Seared Pine Nut Pesto Tofu, 75
Pasilla chile, 180
Pasta
 Live Lasagna, 78
 Manicotti Rustica, 71–72
 Saffron Pasta, 69

 Saffron Ravioli with Wild
 Mushrooms and Cashew Cheese,
 69–70
 Soba Noodles, 105
 Spaghetti and Seitan Wheatballs
 with Roasted Plum Tomato
 Sauce, 94
Peach Parfait, 151
Pears, Balsamic-Caramelized, 36
Pesto, 121
Pesto Marinade, 75
Poblano peppers
 Black Bean and Roasted Poblano
 Soup, 35
 Stuffed Poblano Peppers, 58
Polenta Fries, 104
Pomegranate Cosmo, 168
Potatoes
 Herbed Potato-Leek Soup, 34
 Potato Cakes, 103
 Potato Gnocchi, 73–74
 Roasted Fingerling Potatoes, 102
 Sweet Potato Mash, 101

Q

Quinoa
 about, 180
 Quinoa-Vegetable Pilaf, 107
 Stuffed Avocado with Quinoa
 Pilaf and Chipotle-Avocado
 Dressing, 48

R

Ramps, 180
Raspberry Butter, 138
Red bell peppers
 Butterhead Lettuce, Cauliflower,
 and Red Bell Pepper Salad, 42
 Red Bell Pepper–Curry Sauce, 117
 Roasted Red Bell Pepper and
 Tomato Sauce, 119
Rice
 Arancini with Roasted Plum
 Tomato Sauce, 15
 brown rice vinegar, 179
 Jasmine Rice, 106

Paella, 91–92
    Spring Vegetable Risotto, 61
Ricotta, tofu, 71
Roasted Artichokes with Spring
    Vegetables and Crispy Onion
    Rings, 9–10
Roasted Fingerling Potatoes, 102
Roasted Plum Tomato Sauce, 116
Roasted Red Bell Pepper and Tomato
    Sauce, 119

S
Saffron Pasta, 69
Saffron Ravioli with Wild
    Mushrooms and Cashew Cheese,
    69–70
Sage or Tarragon Aioli, 126
Sages leaves, Jerusalem Artichoke
    Soup with, 33
Sake, 181
Sake Mojito Classico, 174
Salads
    Beet, Fennel, and Fig Salad with
        Cranberry-Sage Dressing, 50
    Blood Orange–Fennel Salad, 52
    Butterhead Lettuce, Cauliflower,
        and Red Bell Pepper Salad, 42
    Heirloom Tomato Salad with
        Macadamia Cheese and Crispy
        Capers, 40
    Kale, Vegetable, and Spelt Berry
        Salad with Chive Vinaigrette, 46
    Mediterranean Salad with
        Kalamata Olive Vinaigrette, 53
    Seaweed Salad with Ginger-
        Sesame Dressing, 49
    Stuffed Avocado with Quinoa
        Pilaf and Chipotle-Avocado
        Dressing, 48
    Watercress, Jicama, and Corn
        Salad with Jalapeño Dressing, 43
    Wild Mushroom and Cipollini
        Salad with Fresh Horseradish
        Dressing, 45
Salsa, Avocado, 11

Sauces
    Apricot Chutney, 125
    Avocado Salsa, 11
    Avocado-Tomatillo Sauce, 76
    Cashew Crème Fraîche, 125
    Chile Sauce, 76
    Chocolate Sauce, 148
    Edamame-Mint Sauce, 124
    Ginger-Soy Dipping Sauce, 115
    Mint-Cilantro Chimichurri
        Sauce, 120
    Mole Sauce, 83
    Peach Topping, 151
    Pesto, 121
    Red Bell Pepper–Curry Sauce, 117
    Roasted Plum Tomato Sauce, 116
    Sage or Tarragon Aioli, 126
    Sofrito Sauce, 87
    Strawberry Sauce, 142
    Tamarind Barbecue Sauce, 89
    Tomato Sauce, 78
    Zucchini Blossom Sauce, 122
Sausage, seitan, 91, 137
Sautéed Royal Trumpet
    Mushrooms, 110
Sautéed Swiss Chard, 113
Sea salt, 181
Seaweed Salad with Ginger-Sesame
    Dressing, 49
Seitan
    about, 181
    Ginger-Seitan Dumplings, 20
    Manicotti Rustica, 71–72
    Nori- and Sesame-Crusted
        Seitan, 84
    Panko-Crusted Seitan
        Milanese, 86
    sausage, 91, 137
    Seitan Cakes, 20
    Seitan Cutlets, 109
    Seitan Piccata, 89
    Sofrito-Seared Seitan, 87
    Spaghetti and Seitan Wheatballs
        with Roasted Plum Tomato
        Sauce, 94
    Tamarind-Barbecued Seitan, 90

Tofu and Seitan Sausage
    Scramble, 137
Tortilla Soup, 30
Side dishes
    about, 99
    Barbecued Black-Eyed Peas, 100
    Braised Green Beans, 111
    Creamed Spinach, 114
    Gingered Sugar Snap Peas, 112
    Granny Smith Coleslaw, 101
    Jasmine Rice, 106
    Marinated Tempeh, 108
    Polenta Fries, 104
    Potato Cakes, 103
    Quinoa-Vegetable Pilaf, 107
    Roasted Fingerling Potatoes, 102
    Roasted Red Bell Pepper and
        Tomato Sauce, 119
    Sautéed Royal Trumpet
        Mushrooms, 110
    Sautéed Swiss Chard, 113
    Seitan Cutlets, 109
    Soba Noodles, 105
    Sweet Potato Mash, 101
Smoked Paprika Hummus, 17
Soba Noodles, 105
Sofrito-Seared Seitan, 87
Sorbets, 146
Soups
    Black Bean and Roasted Poblano
        Soup, 35
    Butternut Squash–Chestnut Soup
        with Caramelized Pears, 36
    Farmers' Market Gazpacho, 29
    Herbed Potato-Leek Soup, 34
    Jerusalem Artichoke Soup with
        Crispy Sage Leaves, 33
    Live Avocado-Cucumber Soup, 26
    Tortilla Soup, 30
Sourdough French Toast, 136
Soy food
    Edamame-Mint Sauce, 124
    soy milk, 181
    vegan buttery spread, 181
    See also Tempeh; Tofu

Spaghetti and Seitan Wheatballs
    with Roasted Plum Tomato
    Sauce, 94
Spelt Berry, Kale and Vegetable
    Salad with Chive Vinaigrette, 46
Spinach, creamed, 114
Spinach-Mushroom Pâté, 19
Spring Vegetable Risotto, 61
Squash
    Butternut Squash, Mushroom,
        and Sage Crepes, 133
    Butternut Squash–Chestnut Soup
        with Caramelized Pears, 36
    Butternut Squash Filling, 70
    Herb-Marinated Grilled
        Vegetables, 64
Strawberry Sauce, 142
Stuffed Avocado with Quinoa
    Pilaf and Chipotle-Avocado
    Dressing, 48
Stuffed Poblano Peppers, 58
Sugar Snap Peas, Gingered, 112
Summer Berry Crumble, 142
Summer Sangria, 165
Sweet Potato Mash, 101

T
Tahini, 181
Tamari, 181
Tamarind, 181
Tamarind-Barbecued Seitan, 90
Tamarind Barbecue Sauce, 89
Tapioca-based cheese, 181
Tarragon or Sage Aioli, 126
Tempeh
    about, 181
    Marinated Tempeh, 108
    tempeh bacon, 15
    Tempeh Cakes, 80–81
    Tempeh with Mole Sauce, 83

Tofu
    about, 181
    Chile-Grilled Tofu with Avocado-
        Tomatillo Sauce, 76
    Chocolate Mousse Tower, 154
    cream cheese, 136
    Creamed Spinach, 114
    Pan-Seared Pine Nut Pesto
        Tofu, 75
    Tofu and Seitan Sausage
        Scramble, 137
    Tofu Cheese, 12
    Tofu Ricotta, 71
Tomatoes
    Arancini with Roasted Plum
        Tomato Sauce, 15
    Farmers' Market Gazpacho, 29
    Heirloom Tomato-Avocado
        Tartare, 6
    Heirloom Tomato Salad with
        Macadamia Cheese and Crispy
        Capers, 40
    Roasted Plum Tomato Sauce, 116
    Roasted Red Bell Pepper and
        Tomato Sauce, 119
    Tomato Sauce, 78
Tortilla Soup, 30

U
Umeboshi vinegar, 181
Unrefined sugar, 181

V
Vanilla Bean Ice Cream, 144
Vanilla Cashew Cream, 151
Vegan buttery spread, 181
Vegan mayonnaise, 181
Vinegar, 179, 181

W
Waffles, Mixed-Grain with
    Raspberry Butter, 138
Wakame, 181
Watercress, Jicama, and Corn Salad
    with Jalapeño Dressing, 43
Wild Mushroom, Asparagus, and
    Spring Vegetable Crepes, 131
Wild Mushroom and Cipollini
    Salad with Fresh Horseradish
    Dressing, 45
Wild Mushroom and Spring
    Vegetable Fricassee, 63
Wine, 55–56, 57
Winter Spiced Sangria, 166

Y
Yuca
    about, 181
    Cashew Cheese-Stuffed Yuca
        Cakes, 18

Z
Zucchini Blossom Sauce, 122
Zucchini Blossom Tempura, 12

MEASUREMENT CONVERSION CHARTS

Volume

U.S.	IMPERIAL	METRIC
1 tablespoon	½ fl oz	15 ml
2 tablespoons	1 fl oz	30 ml
¼ cup	2 fl oz	60 ml
⅓ cup	3 fl oz	90 ml
½ cup	4 fl oz	120 ml
⅔ cup	5 fl oz (¼ pint)	150 ml
¾ cup	6 fl oz	180 ml
1 cup	8 fl oz (⅓ pint)	240 ml
1¼ cups	10 fl oz (½ pint)	300 ml
2 cups (1 pint)	16 fl oz (⅔ pint)	480 ml
2½ cups	20 fl oz (1 pint)	600 ml
1 quart	32 fl oz (1⅔ pints)	1 liter

Weight

U.S./IMPERIAL	METRIC
½ oz	15 g
1 oz	30 g
2 oz	60 g
¼ lb	115 g
⅓ lb	150 g
½ lb	225 g
¾ lb	350 g
1 lb	450 g

Temperature

FAHRENHEIT	CELSIUS/GAS MARK
250°F	120°C/gas mark ½
275°F	135°C/gas mark 1
300°F	150°C/gas mark 2
325°F	160°C/gas mark 3
350°F	180 or 175°C/gas mark 4
375°F	190°C/gas mark 5
400°F	200°C/gas mark 6
425°F	220°C/gas mark 7
450°F	230°C/gas mark 8
475°F	245°C/gas mark 9
500°F	260°C

Length

INCH	METRIC
¼ inch	6 mm
½ inch	1.25 cm
¾ inch	2 cm
1 inch	2.5 cm
6 inches (½ foot)	15 cm
12 inches (1 foot)	30 cm

Library of Congress Cataloging-in-Publication Data

Pierson, Joy.
   The Candle 79 cookbook : modern vegan classics from New York's premier
sustainable restaurant / Joy Pierson, Angel Ramos, and Jorge Pineda ; foreword by
Rory Freedman. — 1st ed.
      p. cm.
   Includes index.
   Summary: "The Candle 79 restaurant expands the horizons of vegan cuisine with
more than 100 healthy, plant-based recipes that are also flavorful and sophisticated, for
conscientious home cooks"— Provided by publisher.
1. Vegan cooking. 2. Candle 79 (Restaurant) 3. Cookbooks. I. Ramos, Angel, 1976-
II. Pineda, Jorge. III. Title.
   TX837.P52928 2011
   641.5'636—dc23
                     2011014509

ISBN 978-1-60774-012-4

Printed in China on paper sourced in accordance with sustainable forest management.

Design by Katy Brown
Prop styling by Lynda White

Author photographs copyright © Eric Marseglia
Vineyard photograph copyright © Heller Estates, Inc.

11 10 9 8 7 6 5 4 3

First Edition